THE USBORNE
INTERNET-LINKED
LIBRARY OF SCIENCE
ENERGY, FORCES
& MOTION

Usborne Publishing has made every
effort to ensure that material on the Web sites
recommended in this book is suitable for its intended
purpose. All the sites in this book have been selected by
Usborne editors as suitable, in their opinion, for children, although
no guarantees can be given. Usborne Publishing is not responsible
for the accuracy or suitability of the information on any Web site
other than its own. We recommend that young children are
supervised while on the Internet, and that children
do not use Internet chat rooms.

ISBN 0-439-44146-3

12 11 10 9 8 7 6 5 4 3 2 1   2 3 4 5 6 7/0

Printed in the U.S.A.   14

First Scholastic printing, October 2002

THE USBORNE
INTERNET-LINKED
LIBRARY OF SCIENCE
ENERGY, FORCES & MOTION

Alastair Smith and Corinne Henderson

Designed by Ruth Russell, Karen Tomlins,
Jane Rigby and Adam Constantine

Digital illustrations by Verinder Bhachu
Digital imagery by Joanne Kirkby

Edited by Laura Howell
Cover design: Nicola Butler
Consultant: Dr Tom Petersen
Web site adviser: Lisa Watts
Editorial assistant: Valerie Modd

Managing designer: Ruth Russell
Managing editor: Judy Tatchell

SCHOLASTIC INC.
New York Toronto London Auckland Sydney
Mexico City New Delhi Hong Kong Buenos Aires

INTERNET LINKS

Throughout this book, we have suggested Web sites where you can find out more about energy, forces and motion. Here are some of the things you can do on the Web sites:

- design your own rollercoaster ride
- test your knowledge of friction by saving an animated skydiver from hitting the ground
- land a virtual spacecraft successfully on the surface of different planets
- find out how much you weigh on any planet

USBORNE QUICKLINKS

To visit the sites in this book, go to the Usborne Quicklinks Web site, where you'll find links to take you to all the sites. Just go to **www.usborne-quicklinks.com** and enter the keywords "science energy".

The links in Usborne Quicklinks are regularly reviewed and updated, but occasionally you may get a message that a site is unavailable. This might be temporary, so try again later, or even the next day. If any of the sites close down, we will, if possible, replace them with suitable alternatives, so you will always find an up-to-date list of sites in Usborne Quicklinks.

WHAT YOU NEED

Some Web sites need additional free programs, called plug-ins, to play sounds, or to show videos, animations or 3-D images. A message will appear on your screen if a site needs a particular plug-in. There is usually a button on the site that you can click on to download it. Alternatively, go to **www.usborne-quicklinks.com** and click on "Net Help". There you can find links to download plug-ins.

INTERNET SAFETY

When using the Internet, please make sure you follow these guidelines:

- Ask your parent's or guardian's permission before you connect to the Internet.
- If a Web site asks you to enter your name, address, e-mail address, telephone number or any other personal details, ask permission from an adult before you type anything.
- If you receive an e-mail from someone you don't know, tell an adult and do not reply to the e-mail.
- Never arrange to meet with anyone you have talked to on the Internet.

NOTES FOR PARENTS

The Web sites described in this book are regularly reviewed and the links in Usborne Quicklinks are updated. However, the content of a Web site may change at any time and Usborne Publishing is not responsible for the content on any Web site other than its own. We recommend that children are supervised while on the Internet, that they do not use Internet Chat Rooms, and that you use Internet filtering software to block unsuitable material. Please ensure that your children read and follow the safety guidelines printed above. For more information, see the "Net Help" area on the Usborne Quicklinks Web site.

DOWNLOADABLE PICTURES

Pictures in this book marked with a ★ symbol may be downloaded from Usborne Quicklinks for your own personal use, for example, to illustrate a homework report or project. The pictures are the copyright of Usborne Publishing and may not be used for any commercial or profit-related purpose.

---

www.usborne-quicklinks.com

Go to Usborne Quicklinks and enter the keywords "science energy" for:

- direct links to all the Web sites in this book
- free downloadable pictures, which appear throughout this book marked with a ★ symbol

---

SEE FOR YOURSELF

The *See for yourself* boxes in this book contain experiments, activities or observations which we have tested. Some recommended Web sites also contain experiments, but we have not tested all of these. This book will be used by readers of different ages and abilities, so it is important that you do not tackle an experiment on your own, either from the book or the Web, that involves equipment that you do not normally use, such as a kitchen knife or stove. Instead, ask an adult to help you.

CONTENTS

ENERGY, FORCES AND MOTION

Physics is the branch of science that deals with matter and energy, the forces that act in the universe, and the results that these forces produce. For instance, when you kick a ball, energy is used to create a force on the ball, which in turn produces motion. This book explains many aspects of energy, forces and motion, and the physical laws which govern them.

These balloons float upward because they are filled with hot air, which always rises. As the air inside them cools, the force of gravity pulls the balloons back down to the ground.

NUCLEAR REACTORS

The energy released by controlled fission reactions can be used to generate electricity, and to power submarines and aircraft carriers.

Nuclear-powered submarine

Engine room

Reactor

Such reactions take place in **nuclear reactors**, such as the pressurized water reactor shown in the diagram at the bottom of the page.

Inside a nuclear reactor, rods made of a radioactive substance such as uranium are bombarded with neutrons*. The nuclei split up, releasing radiation and more neutrons, which set up a chain reaction.

Nuclear power stations generate lots of electricity. However, the used fuel rods remain dangerously radioactive for thousands of years. Disposing of them safely is very difficult.

Nuclear power station

PRESSURIZED WATER REACTOR

A **pressurized water reactor** is one type of nuclear reactor found in power stations. The energy released in the core of the reactor is used to heat water to make steam. The steam turns turbines* that generate electricity.

Nuclear fission reactions take place in the core of the nuclear reactor (1).

The energy released heats pressurized water in the primary water circuit (2).

Heat from the primary water circuit heats the water in the secondary circuit to make steam (3).

Uranium rod

Generator

Steam (3)

Steam-driven turbines (4) generate electricity.

Steam is cooled in the condenser (5) by a supply of water.

Pump

SAFETY FIRST

Nuclear reactions are dangerous to living things. To prevent accidents which would pollute land and air with radiation, the workings in power stations are monitored closely.

Dangerous processes inside a nuclear power station are carefully monitored.

Internet links

Go to **www.usborne-quicklinks.com** for links to the following Web sites:

Web site 1 Discover how radiation is used in science.

Web site 2 The British Nuclear Fuels Ltd Web site.

Web site 3 Facts about nuclear power.

Web site 4 A timeline of nuclear technology.

Web site 5 Advanced and comprehensive information about atomic energy.

Neutrons, 16; Turbines, 49.

FORCES

A **force** is any push or pull on an object. When you pick up an object, you are exerting a force on it. If you leave it sitting where it is, there are still forces acting on it, but they cancel each other out. Forces can make things move faster or slower, stop, change direction, or change size or shape.

The force of gravity makes these dice fall downward.

TYPES OF FORCES

Forces affect objects in many different ways. There are forces you can see, such as a foot kicking a ball, and invisible forces, such as magnetism* and gravity*.

The magnetic force which pulls these tacks to the magnet is an invisible force.

You can see the pulling forces at work in a tug of war. The team that pulls with the most force wins.

See for yourself

Try rolling one ball into another on a smooth surface. The force of your movement will set the ball rolling. The moving ball will exert a force on the stationary one, causing it to move too.

The surface will exert a force (friction*) on both balls, causing them both to slow down, and eventually stop.

A single force acting on an object will make it start to move, or move faster or slower. Two equal forces acting in opposite directions try to change the object's size or shape.

Forces that need two or more objects to be touching each other are called **contact forces**. You are using contact forces when you move an object with your hands.

Some forces don't need objects to be touching. The forces that act at a distance include electric force*, magnetism and the force of gravity.

Compasses work because of the Earth's magnetism*.

The contact force of friction* enables pencils to make marks on paper.

When you kick a ball, the single force of your kick makes the ball start to move.

As you catch a ball, the pushing force of your hands makes the ball slow down and stop.

If you step on a ball, the equal forces of your foot pushing down and the ground pushing up squash it.

A rollercoaster makes use of lots of different forces to gain speed, twist, turn upside down and race along without flying off the track.

When you are on a rollercoaster, you can feel the different forces acting on your body as you are thrown around.

MEASURING FORCES

The strength of a force is measured in **newtons** (**N**), named after the English scientist, Isaac Newton (1642-1727). One newton of force causes a mass of 1kg to accelerate* by one meter per second per second (1m/s^2). This is about the force you would need to lift an empty glass.

A **spring balance** (see right) measures how many newtons a force is exerting. The spring, fixed at one end, is extended (stretched) by the force. **Hooke's law** states that the extension of a material is proportional to the force stretching it. The more the spring stretches, the more newtons the force is applying.

Spring balance

Downward force of weight stretches spring.

The scale gives the strength of the force in newtons.

VECTOR AND SCALAR QUANTITIES

Forces have magnitude (size) and direction. In physics, things that have both these quantities are called **vector quantities**. Acceleration* and velocity* are also vector quantities. A quantity that has magnitude but no direction is called a **scalar quantity**. Temperature, time and mass are examples of scalar quantities. These quantities can be low or high, but they don't have a direction.

Temperature has only magnitude, so it is a scalar quantity.

* Acceleration, Velocity, 29.

Internet links

Go to **www.usborne-quicklinks.com** for links to the following Web sites:

Web site 1 Explore forces as you design your own rollercoaster. Has some useful definitions of physics terms.

Web site 2 This Web site explores more amusement park rides to illustrate the physics of forces.

Web site 3 See the forces involved in skateboarding stunts.

Web site 4 Find out how magnetism works – and learn how to make a compass for yourself.

Web site 5 Information about forces.

COMBINING FORCES

There is usually more than one force acting on an object. For example, a sailboard can experience the forces of gravity, the wind, upthrust and waves. The combined effect is a single force called the **resultant force**. If the strength and direction of all forces is known, you can calculate the resultant force and predict what will happen to the object.

Gravity pushes the board down.

Wind in the sail pushes the board this way.

Waves push the board this way.

Resultant force

Upthrust* from the water pushes the board up.

See for yourself

To see forces of equilibrium in action, try building a tower of cards for yourself.

If you bump a card, the forces acting on the structure will no longer be in equilibrium and the tower will collapse.

Making sure that the forces balance is tricky, because each card depends on others to keep it in place. Cards are so flimsy that a slight knock will unbalance them.

EQUILIBRIUM

There are forces acting on an object even when it is not moving. The forces are all balanced, so they cancel each other out and the object is said to be in **equilibrium**. For example, the force of gravity* pulls down on a tower of cards, while the surface it stands on pushes up with an equal force. The resultant force is zero, so the tower stays in place.

TURNING FORCES

To turn something around a fixed point, for example a door around its hinges, a force with a turning effect is needed. The fixed point is known as a **fulcrum** or **pivot**. It is much easier to turn something around a fulcrum if the force is applied at a distance. This is why a long wrench is more efficient than a shorter one.

It is easiest to undo this bolt by holding the wrench at the end, as the force is then furthest from the fulcrum.

Fulcrum

The force of a turning effect is called a **moment**. The moment around a fulcrum is found by multiplying the strength of the force by its distance from the fulcrum. Moment is measured in **newton meters** (**Nm**) and can be either clockwise or counterclockwise in direction.

1.5m

Lifting force = 10N

Weight = 20N

0.75m

Fulcrum

★

Lifting moment (clockwise):
10N x 1.5m = 15Nm

Weight moment (counterclockwise):
20N x 0.75m = 15Nm

Fulcrum

The picture of the wheelbarrow above shows how turning forces can be in equilibrium just like any other forces. The clockwise moment can cancel out the counterclockwise moment.

* Hooke's law, 21.

ELASTICITY

When forces act on an object that cannot move, they may change its size or shape. Some substances, like rubber, return to their original form when the force is removed. These are called **elastic** substances.

A trampoline is elastic. When the forces stretching it are removed, it goes back to its original shape.

The amount that an elastic substance will stretch obeys Hooke's law*, which states that if the force increases in equal steps, so does the stretch.

If something is stretched beyond its elastic limit, though, Hooke's law no longer works. The **elastic limit** is the point at which a substance alters permanently when it is stretched.

A rubber band is elastic, but will snap if you stretch it too far (that is, beyond its elastic limit).

Some materials do not return to their original form after being stretched and they can hold a new shape. This is called **plastic** behavior.

Modeling clay behaves in a plastic way.

After it has been modeled, the clay keeps the shape that it has been given. This is an example of plastic behavior.

Internet links

Go to **www.usborne-quicklinks.com** for links to the following Web sites:

Web site 1 Take part in an interactive demonstration of moments of force.

Web site 2 Read about the forces that cause the water in a toilet bowl to swirl around.

Web site 3 Find out why balls made of different materials bounce different amounts.

Web site 4 A short article about the life and achievements of scientist Robert Hooke, with links to related scientific information.

DYNAMICS

The study of how forces affect movement is called **dynamics**. The terms inertia and momentum are used to describe how easily objects both start and stop moving. There are three laws of motion which explain the principles governing the movement of all objects. These laws were formulated by the English scientist, Isaac Newton, in 1687.

Isaac Newton, English scientist (1642-1727)

NEWTON'S LAWS OF MOTION

Isaac Newton made important discoveries about many subjects, including motion, gravity and light. His three **laws of motion** have had a major influence on scientific thinking.

Newton's first law states that if an object is not being acted on by a force, it will either stay still or continue moving at a constant speed in a straight line. This is the principle of inertia (see right).

Newton's second law states that any force acting on an object will change its motion. How much change there is depends on the object's mass and the size of the resultant force.

Newton's third law states that when a force acts on an object, the object exerts an equal force in the opposite direction. The first force is called the **action** and the second is the **reaction**.

To start this truck moving, it will take a force to overcome its inertia. (See Newton's first law.)

The same force of wind will move a pine cone less than a leaf because the cone's mass is greater. (See Newton's second law.)

The ball exerts a force on a bat, felt as the slowing down of the bat, that is equal and opposite to the force the bat exerts on the ball. (See Newton's third law.)

INERTIA

Objects resist change in their movement. This tendency, called **inertia**, applies to stationary and moving objects. The inertia of a stationary object makes it hard to get moving. If moving, inertia makes the object want to continue moving in a straight line. It takes a force to overcome inertia.

Without the restraining force of a seatbelt or airbag, the inertia of this crash test dummy would send it through the windshield.

The larger an object's mass, the more inertia it has. A big animal has to exert more force to change its movement than a small one. Twice the mass means twice the inertia.

This adult elephant has five times as much mass as the baby. Its inertia is five times as great.

24

MOMENTUM

Momentum is a measure of an object's tendency to continue moving. It is found by multiplying the object's mass by its velocity. The greater the mass and the velocity, the greater the momentum. Like velocity, momentum is a vector quantity, which means it has both size and direction.

Buzzard

Seagull

If a buzzard and seagull are flying at the same speed, the bird with the greater mass (the buzzard) has greater momentum.

This full cart's mass is 10kg and its velocity is 1m/s east. Its momentum is 10kg m/s east.

An object with a small mass can have the same momentum as an object with a large mass, providing it is moving faster.

This almost empty cart has a mass of 2kg and a velocity of 5m/s east. Its momentum is also 10kg m/s east.

See for yourself

Contraptions called Newton's cradles are sometimes sold as interesting, grown-up "toys" which show conservation of momentum. See if you can find one. As the first ball hits the other balls, its momentum is transferred through to the last ball, making it move.

CONSERVATION OF MOMENTUM

When two objects collide, such as the pink ball and the blue ball shown here, their total momentum stays the same as it was just before the collision. This is called the **law of conservation of momentum**. So when one object loses momentum in a collision, the other gains the same amount.

The pink ball rolls towards the blue ball.

As the pink ball hits the blue ball, it transfers momentum through the blue ball to the red ball.

As their masses are the same, the red ball accelerates to the speed that the pink ball had before the collision.

Internet links

Go to **www.usborne-quicklinks.com** for links to the following Web sites:

Web site 1 The principles of physics associated with baseball.

Web site 2 See how momentum is passed on from one object to another.

Web site 3 Browse a library of biographies of famous scientists, including Newton and Pascal.

Web site 4 Another collection of biographies of famous scientists.

Web site 5 An advanced explanation of Newton's three laws of motion.

FRICTION

When a moving object is touching another object, like a coin sliding across a table, the moving object slows down. The force that causes this is called **friction**. The rougher the surfaces are, and the harder they press together, the more friction there will be. Friction occurs in liquids and gases as well as between solids. Anything that experiences friction warms up.

New shoe

Old shoe

Constant friction with the floor means a ballet dancer's shoes wear out after a few weeks.

USING FRICTION

Friction is useful in some situations and a nuisance in others. If there were no friction between surfaces, it would be impossible to grip anything.

Many kinds of machines make use of friction. With too little friction between tires and the surface of a road, for example, drivers wouldn't be able to stop their vehicles from sliding around.

The skis' smooth undersides minimize friction with the snow, allowing them to slide very easily. However, their sharp edges create friction when the skier turns, enabling him to control his speed and direction.

Water and mud on the road reduce friction because they act as lubricants (see opposite page). The grooves on a tire channel water or mud through them, so that the raised rubber pieces (the **tread**) can grip the surface of the road.

Some devices need friction to be able to work at all. For example, friction between a match and a matchbox generates enough heat for chemicals in the match head to burn. All brakes work by using friction to slow down a vehicle's wheels.

Disc brake

Brake pad

Brake pads press against this steel wheel, causing enough friction to slow it down.

The soles of hiking shoes are made from materials, such as rubber, which provide a lot of friction.

REDUCING FRICTION

Lots of friction between machine parts is damaging. It causes wear and tear, and some of the energy needed to run the machine is wasted on heat instead of movement. Oil is used to reduce friction because it is smoother than any solid surface, so it allows objects to slide across each other more easily. A liquid used like this is called a **lubricant**.

Metal — Oil — Metal

Magnification shows how a smooth-seeming metal surface is actually fairly rough. A layer of oil between moving metal surfaces reduces friction.

A layer of **ball bearings** between two surfaces in a machine reduces the amount of contact between the surfaces. This reduces the friction between them, and the amount of wear.

Ball bearings lie around the axle of this wheel. They rotate as the wheel turns.

FRICTION IN AIR AND SPACE

Drag, or **air resistance**, is the friction that occurs between air and any object moving through it (see also page 44). In space, there is no air, so there is no friction. The Space Shuttle, for instance, experiences no friction as it moves through space, until it re-enters the Earth's atmosphere.

Drag slows down the Shuttle as it enters the Earth's atmosphere. The friction between the Shuttle and the air makes it glow red hot.

See for yourself

You can see how ball bearings reduce friction using some marbles and a big book. First, push the book along on its own. Notice the friction. Now put marbles under the book and push again. The marbles roll between the book and the surface, reducing friction.

Marble

STREAMLINING

To reduce drag, vehicles are designed so that they are **streamlined**. Streamlining lets the air flow over a vehicle in smooth lines, so that it can move forwards with less effort.

Car manufacturers use jets of smoke to test the streamlining of new cars. Here, the Ford Ka is being tested.

FRICTION IN WATER

Water is denser* than air, so more friction acts on objects moving through water. Fish, and sea mammals such as whales, have naturally streamlined bodies that reduce the friction between themselves and the water.

Water flows easily over a whale's streamlined body.

Internet links

Go to **www.usborne-quicklinks.com** for links to the following Web sites:

Web site 1 Discover the scientific principles behind cycling, showing the importance of friction in the sport.

Web site 2 Read about the scientific principles behind ice hockey.

Web site 3 Play an entertaining game to find out the effect of air friction on your body. Get it wrong and disaster will follow.

Web site 4 Find out how you can build a simple working model hovercraft.

Web site 5 A friction experiment using a toy car.

* Density, 40.

MOTION

I n physics, **motion** is the study of how something moves, whether it is a planet moving around the Sun or a snowboarder flying through the air. An object's motion is usually described in terms of its velocity and acceleration, and its motion only changes if a force, or several forces, act on it.

Snowboarders can reach speeds of 22m/s, which is the same as 50mph.

SPEED

Speed is a measure of how fast an object is moving. The average speed of a moving object can be calculated by dividing the distance it has traveled by the time it has taken to do so.

Speed calculation

This cyclist has gone 500yds in 40 seconds. The calculation below gives her average speed.

$$\text{Average speed} = \frac{\text{Distance (yards)}}{\text{Time (seconds)}}$$

$$= \frac{500}{40} = 12.5\text{yds/s}$$

Speed is a scalar quantity. This means that it measures the amount of speed a moving object has, but not the direction in which it is moving. In physics, the unit of measurement most often used is meters per second (m/s). However, you will often see miles per hour (mph) as well. This measures how far something will go in an hour.

CHANGING SPEED

The speed of a moving object can change from moment to moment. A sprinter, for instance, runs slowest when setting off at the start of a race. He is likely to be running fastest as he approaches the finishing line. The speed of something at any particular moment is called its **instantaneous speed**.

For example, in 1999 the men's world record for the 100m race was 9.84 seconds. This is an average speed of 10.16m/s. After running 1m of the race, though, the winner's instantaneous speed might have been 3m/s. After a few more meters, it could have been as high as 11m/s.

Sprinters during a race

VELOCITY

Velocity measures the direction in which an object is traveling as well as its speed. This makes velocity a vector quantity. The velocity of a moving object can change even if its speed remains exactly the same because a change in direction changes the velocity.

Although this car is traveling at a steady speed of 10km/h (6mph), its velocity is changing all the time because it is constantly changing direction.

Path of car

Velocity is measured in meters per second (m/s) in a particular direction. For instance, someone walking north at 1.5m/s has a velocity of 1.5m/s north. **Relative velocity** is the velocity a moving object appears to have when viewed from another moving object.

These stunt jets are both flying at a velocity of 83m/s in the same direction.

The velocity of one jet relative to the other (from the point of view of either) is zero.

ACCELERATION

Acceleration is a change in the velocity of an object, that is, a change in its speed or direction in a given time. In physics, acceleration is measured in meters per second per second, or m/s^2. This is not as confusing as it looks. If something accelerates at $1m/s^2$ (1 meter per second per second), it gets faster by one meter a second, every second.

A decrease in velocity is called **negative acceleration**, or **deceleration**. Any change in speed or direction means that an object accelerates, or decelerates, as both affect velocity. Car manufacturers usually consider acceleration in kilometers (or miles) per hour per second. This is simply using different units to measure the same thing.

If a car is traveling at a steady 50km/h (30mph) in one direction, its acceleration is zero. This is because neither its speed nor direction change.

This Porsche 911 Turbo accelerates from 0-100km/h (0-60mph) in 4.5 seconds. This works out at an average acceleration of $6.2m/s^2$.

When they first leave the plane, the Earth's gravity causes skydivers to accelerate at a rate of $9.8m/s^2$.

When skydivers open their parachutes, they suddenly decelerate.

See for yourself

Make three small balls using modeling clay. Drop each one from a different height. The greater the drop, the bigger the dent in the ball when it hits the floor. This is because the further things fall, the faster they go.

The ball on the left falls furthest, so it is most squashed when it lands.

Internet links

Go to **www.usborne-quicklinks.com** for links to the following Web sites:

Web site 1 Lots of practical information about speed.

Web site 2 Definition of motion and articles on "Types of Motion" and "The Laws of Motion and Relativity".

Web site 3 An online converter of units of measurement.

Web site 4 Skateboarding explained by a scientist.

Web site 5 Concise explanations of velocity and acceleration.

TERMINAL VELOCITY

When something falls through a gas or liquid it accelerates, at a decreasing rate, until it reaches its maximum constant velocity. This is called its **terminal velocity**.

As an example, imagine skydivers jumping from a plane. They start to accelerate the moment they jump from the plane.

They continue accelerating, but at a slower and slower rate, until they reach a speed of about 200km/h (125mph). At this point they stop accelerating.

When the acceleration has dropped to zero, they have reached their terminal velocity.

When something begins to fall, it accelerates quickly.

The longer it falls, the less quickly it accelerates.

When it stops accelerating. It has reached its terminal velocity.

RESISTANCE

The pull of **gravity** is the force that makes an object accelerate downward. But as the object starts to move, it experiences **resistance**, an upward force, from the gas or liquid it is falling through. The faster the object falls, the stronger the resistance becomes, until it equals the downward force of the weight of the object. The object stops accelerating at this point and has reached its terminal velocity.

The terminal velocity of an object is slower in a liquid than it is in a gas. This is because a liquid provides more resistance than a gas. As a result, the forces become balanced earlier and the object stops accelerating sooner.

A falling coin takes longer to reach its terminal velocity in air than in water.

MOTION IN A CIRCLE

All moving objects try to travel in a straight line (see Newton's first law, page 24). The force which makes something turn in a circle instead is called a **centripetal force**. This is any force that constantly pulls toward the center of a circle.

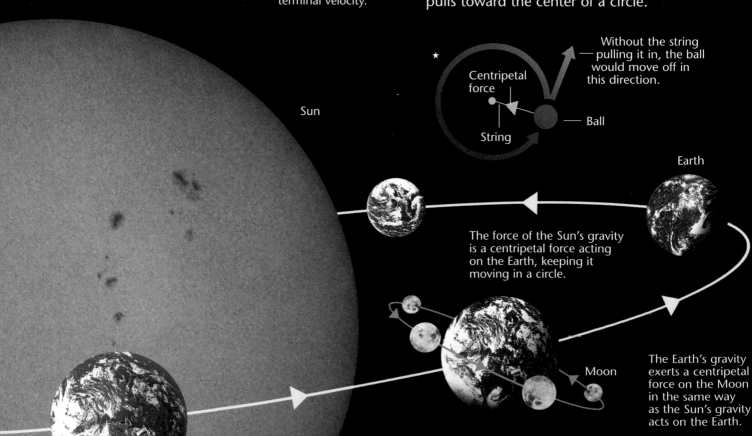

Without the string pulling it in, the ball would move off in this direction.

Centripetal force

String

Ball

Sun

The force of the Sun's gravity is a centripetal force acting on the Earth, keeping it moving in a circle.

Earth

Moon

The Earth's gravity exerts a centripetal force on the Moon in the same way as the Sun's gravity acts on the Earth.

CENTRIPETAL FORCE - AN EXAMPLE

If you tie a small object to a piece of string and whirl it around your head, the pull of the string on the object is a centripetal force. As long as you whirl fast enough, the object will not fall in on you. If you let go of the string, you remove the centripetal force and the object will fly off at a tangent, as when an athlete throws the "hammer".

1. The athlete pulls on the wire to make the hammer move.

2. His pull is a centripetal force on the hammer as it moves.

3. The faster the hammer moves, the more centripetal force is needed.

4. The hammer flies off when the centripetal force is removed.

GYROSCOPES

Gyroscopes are wheels that can spin very fast within a frame. The centripetal force created means that the frame can resist the force of gravity. It can even tilt steeply without toppling over. However, when the wheel slows, the gyroscope will fall. (You can buy gyroscopes in some toy stores.)

Frame ————————

Wheel ————

Frame ————————————

This gyroscope resists gravity when spinning. It can stand on the end of a bar, which is attached to the frame directly beneath the middle of the spinning wheel.

Bar ————

See for yourself

You can see the effect of centripetal force for yourself.

Put a marble in a plastic bowl and move the bowl so that the marble moves in a circle. You have created a centripetal force on the marble.

However, the marble will fly out of the bowl when it reaches a certain speed. The centripetal force is not strong enough to keep it moving in such a tight circle.

Notice that the marble flies off in a straight line.

Internet links

Go to **www.usborne-quicklinks.com** for links to the following Web sites:

Web site 1 Concise explanations of the concepts that govern the physics of motion.

Web site 2 Find out how a bicycle wheel can behave like a big gyroscope.

Web site 3 Learn more about the physics of bicycle wheels.

Web site 4 Play an interactive game in which you must control different forces to get a cannon ball to hit a target.

Web site 5 Read about, and listen to, details about Aristotle's, Galileo's and Newton's ideas on motion. Then take the online quiz.

Web site 6 Detailed, advanced explanations of velocity and acceleration.

Web site 7 A useful encyclopedia article defining force.

GRAVITY

The force of **gravity** attracts objects to each other. This attraction is not noticeable unless one of the objects is very large, such as a planet. The area within which gravity has an effect is called a **gravitational field**. The Earth and Moon both have gravitational fields, although the Earth's is a lot stronger than the Moon's because it is a much bigger object.

The force of the Sun's gravity keeps a belt of rocks, called asteroids, orbiting around it.

GRAVITY AND MASS

The strength of the pull of gravity between two objects depends on how far apart they are and their masses. **Mass** is the amount of matter that an object contains and this never varies. Any two objects, such as two tomatoes, are attracted to each other, but as their masses are small, the force of gravity between them is tiny and there is no visible effect.

The attraction between these small objects is so tiny that it cannot be felt.

EARTH'S GRAVITY

The force of gravity between the Earth and anything on it is extremely noticeable because the mass of the Earth is so large.

The pull of the Earth's gravity makes any object, such as this conker, fall to the ground.

GRAVITY AND WEIGHT

Weight is a measure of the pull of gravity on an object's mass. The further away an object is from the center of the Earth, the less the pull of gravity on it. Because of this, you weigh slightly less at a high altitude (for example, at the top of a high mountain) than at the bottom, even though your mass stays the same.

When they are space walking, astronauts weigh far less than they do on Earth. They are so far from the Earth's center that the planet's gravity has little effect on them.

CENTER OF GRAVITY

Gravity affects every part of an object, but there is one point where the object's whole weight seems to act. This is its **center of gravity**. An object can often be balanced at its center of gravity.

X = center of gravity

Regularly shaped and symmetrical objects, like this handweight, have their center of gravity exactly in the middle.

A **stable object** returns to its original position when tilted. Center of gravity is the key to stability. If an object tilts, but its center of gravity remains above its base, it won't fall over.

A race car is very stable. Its center of gravity is low and its base is wide.

An **unstable object** has its center of gravity high up, and has a relatively narrow base. If an unstable object is tilted, its center of gravity soon stops being above its base.

A stationary motorcycle is a good example of an unstable object. It will soon fall over when it is tilted.

Tall, narrow things aren't necessarily unstable. For example, a double-decker bus is built so that its center of gravity is low, making it stable.

The bottom part of the bus is heavy, containing the engine, wheels and chassis. The top part of the bus is light. As a result, the center of gravity is low.

See for yourself

Follow these steps to find the center of gravity of a piece of paper.

1. Hold up the paper and let it dangle.

2. Hold it against a wall and draw a line straight down the paper from where you are holding it.

3. Hold the paper at a different point and repeat step 2. The center of gravity will be where the lines cross. If you repeat this, the lines should cross in the same place.

Stable object   **X** = center of gravity

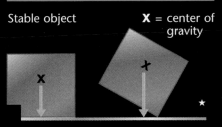

Unless a stable object is tilted a very long way, its center of gravity stays above its base. As a result, it tends to fall back onto its base.

Unstable object   **X** = center of gravity

When an unstable object is tilted, its center of gravity quickly stops being above its base. This causes the object to topple over.

Tall, stable object   **X** = center of gravity

With a low center of gravity, the tall object must tilt a long way before it topples.

EARTH AND MOON

As the Moon goes around the Earth, its gravity pulls at the planet. This has an effect on the seas of the Earth, which rise and fall. Areas where the water has risen are having a **high tide**. Areas that are not having a high tide are having a **low tide**.

The Moon's effect on the tides

High tide

Moon

Pull of Moon

High tide

Low tides occur half-way between high tides.

Similarly, the Earth's gravity also pulls at the Moon. It is providing the force, called centripetal force, which is needed to keep the Moon locked in orbit around the Earth itself.

For more information on centripetal force, see *Motion in a Circle*, on page 30.

PRESSURE

A needle will go through a piece of cloth, but with the same amount of force, a pencil will not. The differently shaped points of the needle and pencil exert different amounts of pressure. Pressure is everywhere. It operates many machines and affects our weather. Solids, liquids and gases all apply pressure to the surfaces they touch.

Sharp scissors cut well because the blades exert pressure over a tiny area.

WHAT IS PRESSURE?

When a force acts on an object it exerts **pressure**. The pressure acts at a right-angle to the object itself, and its strength depends on the amount of force and the area over which it is applied. For example, someone walking on soft snow will sink into it in normal shoes but not if they wear snowshoes. The person's weight is the same but snowshoes spread the weight over a larger area. This reduces the pressure.

The bottom of a snowshoe is about six times bigger than the sole of a foot.

ATMOSPHERIC PRESSURE

Atmospheric pressure is the weight of air pressing down on the Earth's surface. Over one square meter, the weight of air pressing down is heavier than a large elephant. Air pressure is greatest near the ground, and reduces with height. At 35,000ft above the ground, where jets fly, air pressure is very low as there is less air pressing down on anything up there. Less air means less oxygen, and aircraft have pressurized cabins so that people can breathe. The air pressure inside the plane is kept roughly the same as it would be at ground level.

Pressure is measured in **pascals (Pa)**, which are named after the French scientist Blaise Pascal (1623-1662), who made many discoveries about air pressure.

CHANGING WEATHER

Atmospheric pressure is measured in **millibars (mb)**. Weather changes as the pressure changes, with low pressure signaling bad weather and high pressure bringing a settled, fine spell. For example, usual atmospheric pressure at sea level is 1,013mb. However, this can fall to 910mb in a hurricane.

Heavy rains and strong winds are brought by low atmospheric pressure.

PRESSURE IN FLUIDS

Fluids (liquids and gases) change shape according to the container that they are in. The pressure inside them acts outward in all directions.

Air inside a beach ball pushes out in all directions, keeping it blown up.

Liquid in a glass exerts pressure against the sides as well as the bottom.

HYDRAULIC MACHINES

Hydraulic machines are machines powered by liquid pressure. A liquid cannot be squashed, so if you press one part of the liquid, pressure increases throughout and the liquid has to move somewhere.

This robot arm works using hydraulic pressure.

Car brakes are hydraulic. Brake fluid is pushed through the brake system, forcing the wheels to slow down.

How a car's footbrake works

Driver presses pedal, pushing piston (1) which forces fluid through cylinder (2). Fluid goes down pipe into two more cylinders (red arrows). These press brake pads (3) against disc in wheel. Friction* slows down wheel (4).

PNEUMATIC MACHINES

Pneumatic machines are driven by the pressure of gases, usually air. Unlike liquid, air can be compressed into a smaller space, and this increases its pressure.

A pneumatic drill, for example, is powered by a piston which squashes air inside the drill to a very high pressure. The compressed air pushes out with enough force to power the drill to crack rock.

Pneumatic drill

A foam and water fire extinguisher is a pneumatic machine which uses compressed carbon dioxide gas.

How a fire extinguisher works

Squeezing handle (1) releases carbon dioxide gas from canister (2). Gas pushes down on a mixture of water and detergent (3), forcing it up a tube (4) and through a hose (5). It shoots out as a jet of foam and water.

See for yourself

This experiment shows how air pushes out in all directions. You need a lightweight book and a plastic bag.

Put the book on the bag and blow into the bag.

Air pressure increases inside the bag and lifts the book.

Internet links

Go to **www.usborne-quicklinks.com** for links to the following Web sites:

Web site 1 Find out about the effect that pressure has on underwater divers.

Web site 2 Learn how pressure is used to power hydraulic machines, from dump trucks to log splitters.

Web site 3 Discover how water towers work using pressure.

Web site 4 Find out how pressure helps the giant squid use the suckers on its tentacles.

Web site 5 Simple explanations of pressure in a gas or a liquid.

* Friction, 26.

SIMPLE MACHINES

All machines make physical work easier to do by taking the effort needed to operate them and using it in a more efficient way. Simple machines are devices such as levers and screws. Complex machines, such as drills and cranes, are made up of combinations of simple machines.

The wheel, one of the most important devices ever invented, forms the basis of many machines.

OVERCOMING LOAD

To move any object, you need to overcome a force called the **load**, which is often the weight of the object. A simple machine helps you to do this by taking the force of your **effort** and applying it more efficiently.

The effort is the force that turns the handle.

The effort applied at the handle creates a greater force here, enabling the screwdriver to overcome the load applied by the screw.

It is possible to find out how much more force a simple machine provides compared with the amount of effort that is put in. This is done by dividing the load by the amount of effort used, and is called the **force ratio**.

The load exerted by the nutshell is 4N. But squeezing the nutcracker handles to crack it only takes 1N. So the force ratio is 4:1.

If a force ratio is 4:1, the load which the machine overcomes is four times greater than the effort used. Machines like this are called **force magnifiers**.

LEVERS

A **lever** is a rod that turns at a fixed point, called a **fulcrum**, making it easier to perform a task. There are three classes of levers, each with a different arrangement of the fulcrum, effort and load.

A **class one lever** has the fulcrum between the effort and the load.

Fulcrum

Effort

Load

Load (4N)

Fulcrum

A **class two lever** has the load between the effort and the fulcrum.

Effort (1N)

Effort

A **class three lever** has the effort between the load and the fulcrum.

Fulcrum

Load

The further the effort is from the fulcrum, the easier a lever is to use, so longer levers are generally more useful. (See *Turning Forces* on page 23.)

WHEELS

When a **wheel** turns a rod (such as a steering wheel turning a steering column in a car) the force applied on the wheel is turned into a bigger force by the rod. The bigger the wheel is, the more easily the rod turns.

Turning the steering wheel exerts a big enough force at the steering column to turn a car's front wheels.

Steering column

When an axle is turned, a wheel connected to it will convert the axle's circular motion into a straight line motion that can move loads across the ground. A car's wheels are an example of this. The wheel turns further than the axle because it is bigger.

See for yourself

To see how a class one lever works, put a pencil under the middle of a rigid ruler. Put a lightweight book on one end.

Book

Ruler

Press down to raise book.

Load

Fulcrum (pencil)

Effort

Try changing the position of the pencil under the ruler. The further the effort is from the fulcrum, the easier it is to lift the load.

PULLEYS

Pulleys help to lift heavy loads and are often used in lifts and cranes. The load is attached to a rope which passes around one or more grooved wheels. When the other end of the rope is pulled, the load is lifted.

Pulley

Pulleys let you pull down instead of up, so you can use your weight to help.

The more wheels a pulley has, the easier it is to lift a load, as the weight of the load is spread out over more rope.

This crane works like a giant pulley. The rope is made of strong steel cable. The pulling strength is provided by the crane's engine.

SCREWS

A **screw** has an axle and a thread which work together like an inclined plane (see below) wrapped around a cylinder. The axle is the cylinder and the thread the inclined plane.

The turning screw converts the force applied into a much greater straight line force. As a result, the axle easily drives straight into the object.

A corkscrew converts a turning motion into a straight line force.

The strong steel cable passes over grooved wheels.

The cable can lift very heavy objects, such as steel and concrete building materials.

GEARS

Gears are used to change speed in many different kinds of complex machines, from cars to clocks. They do this by changing the size of a turning force.

Gears consist of two or more toothed wheels, or **cogs**, that fit into each other, so that turning one cog turns the other. A large cog makes a smaller one turn faster.

This gear changes the size and direction of the turning force.

This clock works using a complicated system of geared wheels.

The crane's engine is housed here.

Internet links

Go to **www.usborne-quicklinks.com** for links to the following Web sites:

Web site 1 Find out why bikes are such an efficient form of transportation.

Web site 2 Raise an obelisk using a simple machine.

Web site 3 Read about Leonardo da Vinci and some of the machines that he invented.

Web site 4 Find out more about gears.

Web site 5 Learn more about pulleys.

Web site 6 Read more about cranes.

INCLINED PLANES

An **inclined plane** is just a slope, like a ramp. It is easier to move an object up an inclined plane than vertically upward, because you travel further, so less force is needed for the same amount of work.

80ft slope

10ft vertical

If you push an object eight times as far up an inclined plane as lifting it straight up, you only need one eighth of the force.

USING SIMPLE MACHINES

Simple machines can be used to make up more complex machines. Here are some examples. Even animals, such as the lobster on the right, can have body parts which work in the same way as a machine.

Propellers are a simple form of screw. They are used to push ships through water – and to pull aircraft through the air.

Archimedes' screw was an early device for pumping water from rivers or lakes.

Handle

Water was drawn up on the inclined planes of a turning screw.

Big gear wheel

Small gear wheel

Handle

Gears on a whisk increase the size of the turning force needed to move the handle, so that the blades can be turned very fast.

Blades

Drill bit

Gears   Drive shaft

An electric drill combines gears and a screw at the tip, called a **bit**. The gears change the speed at which the bit rotates, so that it can drill a hole quickly or slowly.

A motor provides power to a system of gears and wheels which move the stairs and handrails on an escalator.

Scissors are class one levers. The blades are sharp wedges that force surfaces apart.

Fulcrum

A fan is a third class lever. When you wave it, your wrist acts as the fulcrum.

The Ancient Egyptians, who built the pyramids, may have used inclined planes, in the form of spiral slopes, to push enormous blocks of stone up into place. The tallest pyramids were about 480ft high. ★

Fulcrum

A lobster's claws, or pincers, are third class levers.

An ax turns a downward force into a sideways cutting force. The blade is a **wedge** that pushes apart as it cuts down.

Your front teeth, called incisors, are wedges. They work like axes, pushing food apart as they cut down.

Downward force

Sideways force

WORK AND POWER

In science, the word "work" has a particular meaning. **Work** is done when a force makes an object move. Work is only done when the object moves.

MEASURING WORK

Work transfers energy from one object to another and, like energy, is measured in **joules (J)**. One joule equals the work done (and energy transferred) when a force of 1 newton (N) moves an object 1 meter in the direction of the force.

If this man pushes the box with a force of 100 newtons for 3 meters, he performs 300 joules of work.

POWER

Power is the rate at which work is done, or energy is transferred. It is measured in **watts (W)**, named after James Watt, and is worked out by dividing the work done by the time taken to do it.

It takes twice as much power to move the box 3 meters in one minute as to move it 3 meters in two minutes.

AN EXAMPLE OF WORK

In the picture, the male dancer's lifting force is overcoming the force of gravity, and work is being done as he raises the ballerina in the air.

The male dancer is using his energy to lift the ballerina. Most of this energy is being converted to potential energy* in the dancer in the air. Also, some heat energy is being released by the male dancer's body.

The ballerina has to do work as she moves her body into the correct pose.

See for yourself

You can measure how much work you do (in joules) when you go upstairs by measuring the height of the stairs and multiplying it by your weight in newtons (your weight in kilograms† x 10). Divide the work you do by the time it takes to do it to find out how much power you exert (in watts). The quicker you go, the more power you exert.

Height of stairs

Internet links

Go to **www.usborne-quicklinks.com** for links to the following Web sites:

Web site 1 A clear explanation of what physicists mean by "work".

Web site 2 Find out how much work your body does. (Answers are in calories. Joules = calories x 4.19)

Web site 3 Read a short biography of inventor James Watt.

Web site 4 A definition of power and its relationship to work.

* Potential energy, 8.

† To find your weight in kilograms, multiply your weight in pounds by 0.45.

FLOATING

Why do some substances float in water, but not others? And why are there so few substances that are able to float in air? By understanding the principles of floating (and sinking), engineers can build ships out of metals that are heavier than the water they float in, and design airships and hot-air balloons that can float in the air.

WHY THINGS FLOAT

When an object is put into water, it pushes aside, or **displaces**, some of the water. It takes up the space where the water was, and the level of the water rises.

According to legend, the Ancient Greek scientist Archimedes (287-212BC) first realized how objects displace water when he got into his bath.

This is a medieval picture of Archimedes making his discovery.

Water pushes back against an object placed in it with a force called **upthrust**. If this is the same as the weight of the object, the object floats. The weight of the object and the weight of the water it displaces are equal.

Hot-air balloons are filled with air that is lighter than the cool air outside them. They rise up because hot air floats.

ARCHIMEDES' PRINCIPLE

Archimedes' principle states that the upthrust acting on an object is equal to the weight of the fluid that the object displaces. An object will sink into a fluid, such as water, and keep on sinking unless the force of the upthrust from the fluid becomes equal to the weight of the object.

Water is displaced (yellow arrows) as boat is lowered. Upthrust (red arrow) pushes back on boat.

When upthrust of water equals weight of boat, boat settles on water and floats steadily.

DENSITY

One object may float while another of the same size may sink. Same-sized objects have different weights if their density is different. **Density** is a measure of the amount of matter in an object (its **mass**) compared to its volume (size).

A steel ball is heavier than an apple of the same size because it is denser. Its matter is packed more tightly together. The apple floats (just) in water but the steel ball sinks.

FLOATING IN THE AIR

Air, like water, pushes back at an object with a force called upthrust. This equals the weight of air pushed aside by the object. If the upthrust equals the weight of the object, the object floats. But air is so light that few things float in it. Hot-air balloons and helium-filled airships can both float in air, though, because hot air and helium are both lighter than cold air.

This cutaway drawing shows an airship filled with helium gas, which is lighter than air.

Airships are built so that the helium is held in a series of separate cells. If one cell bursts, only the helium in that section will be lost.

Helium gas cell

Metal frames give the airship a stable shape.

HOW SHIPS FLOAT

Modern ships are made of steel, which is eight times denser than water. But they don't sink because their overall density is lower than water. This is because ships are hollow. All the space inside them makes them less dense than water. Their huge volume pushes aside (or displaces) a large amount of water and so creates a lot of upthrust on the ship.

Even when fully laden, a container ship still displaces so much water that it floats. The displaced water creates a massive upthrust on the huge ship.

RELATIVE DENSITIES

For an object to float in water, its density needs to be less than, or the same as, the density of water. If not, the water cannot provide enough upthrust to support it.

The **relative density** of an object is its density when compared to the density of water. The relative density of water is 1, so an object will sink if its relative density is more than 1, but float if it is 1 or less.

Water 1 Cork 0.2 Air 0.0012

Aluminum 2.7 Steel 8 Copper 9

This picture shows the relative densities of different substances. Nearly all metals are denser than water.

See for yourself

You can use a ball of modeling clay to show how a ship floats. If you drop the ball into water it will sink. This is because the ball is denser than the water. If you shape the same piece of clay into a hollow bowl, though, it should float.

Although it is the same weight as the ball, the bowl floats because it pushes aside more water. The force of the upthrust equals its weight.

Bowl-shaped clay floats.

Ball of clay sinks.

Internet links

Go to **www.usborne-quicklinks.com** for links to the following Web sites:

Web site 1 Find out about gases, density and buoyancy. Includes pictures and videos.

Web site 2 The Web site of the Breitling Orbiter, the first hot-air balloon to circle Earth non-stop.

Web site 3 Learn about buoyancy, with an experiment and links to more activities.

Web site 4 Find out how airships fly.

Web site 5 Various activities relating to balloons.

SHIPS AND BOATS

Ships and boats once relied on the wind or human strength for their power. The invention of engines meant that propellers* could be used to drive ships through the water. More recent boat designs include hydrofoils and hovercraft.

Viking ship

In the ninth century, the Vikings used ships like this. For power, they used sails as well as oars.

Tankers

Tankers carry oil or other liquid cargo in tanks. Big tankers, called supertankers, are the largest ships in the world.

Helicopter landing pad

Control deck

Hovercraft

A hovercraft (also called an Air-Cushion Vehicle, or ACV) skims over the water on a cushion of air inside a rubber skirt.

Rudders

Fins

Engines

Propellers drive the hovercraft forward.

Control cabin

Cutaway view of rubber skirt

Cruise ships

Large, luxurious cruise ships are designed to carry hundreds of people on vacations.

Container ships

Container ships carry goods in large metal boxes. These can be unloaded or loaded quickly by cranes. One ship can carry hundreds of containers.

Containers

Hydrofoils

Hydrofoils have stilts attached to underwater "wings" called foils. When a hydrofoil speeds up, its hull lifts out of the water, reducing water resistance. Two designs of foil are surface-piercing foils and ladder foils.

Hull

Surface-piercing foil

Hydrofoil with surface-piercing foils

Hydrofoil with ladder foils

Iron ship

This nineteenth century boat had sails and a steam engine that drove a propeller (shown with the rudder in the circle). It had an iron hull.

Clipper

Clippers were used in the nineteenth century to carry goods around the world. They had so many sails that they could reach speeds of nearly 25mph.

Racing yacht

This old racing yacht was built using heavy wood, and has weighty canvas sails. Modern versions use more lightweight materials, so they are faster and easier to steer.

SUBMARINES

Submarines can dive and surface by altering their relative density*. They carry large containers called **ballast tanks**. When air is expelled from these tanks and replaced with water, the submarine's density increases and it dives. When it needs to surface, air is pumped back into the tanks and water is forced back out. This makes the submarine less dense, and it rises to the surface.

— Periscope

The ballast tanks are placed between the submarine's two hulls.

A submarine dives as its ballast tanks are filled with water.

Outer hull

Inner hull

A submarine rises as air is pumped back into the tanks and water is forced out.

Submarines have powerful propellers to drive them through the water. Some have engines driven by nuclear power.

Propeller

See for yourself

Put the top on an empty plastic bottle and hold it under water. Let it go and the bottle will shoot up to the surface.

Now fill the bottle with water. You are making the bottle denser, so it will now remain underwater, just like a submarine with water in its ballast tanks.

Internet links

Go to **www.usborne-quicklinks.com** for links to the following Web sites:

Web site 1 Information about ships, maps, navigation and the science of sailing, from historical times to the modern day.

Web site 2 Take a virtual tour around a submarine on PBS TV's *Submarines, Secrets and Spies* Web site.

Web site 3 Learn about the history of ships and shipbuilding.

Web site 4 Look at old warships at the Historic Dockyard in Portsmouth, UK.

Web site 5 Explore an ancient seaport and shipyard in Connecticut, USA.

* Relative density, 41.

FLIGHT

The first powered flight took place a century ago and lasted only twelve seconds. Now planes can travel faster than the speed of sound, and helicopters can hover in the air without moving. The wings of planes and the blades of helicopters have a special shape which helps them to fly.

Kites were the first things that people managed to fly.

HOW PLANES FLY

Planes can fly because of the shape of their wings. The wings are curved on top and flatter underneath. A bird's wings have the same shape. It is called an **airfoil**.

Cross section of an airfoil shape

Curved on top

Flow of air

Flatter underneath

★

The air above an airfoil wing has further to travel than the air under it. When the flow of a gas such as air gets faster, its pressure is reduced. This is called **Bernoulli's principle**. Because of this, the slower air flowing under the wing has a higher pressure and pushes up on it. This force is called **lift**, and it causes the wing to rise up into the air.

Cross section of an aircraft wing

Wing pushed up by higher air pressure underneath.

Air travels faster over the wing.

Air travels slower under the wing.

★

Air is divided by the wing's leading edge.

Gliders are very light and the lift from their wings is strong enough to overcome the downward pull of gravity. Heavier aircraft need a force called **thrust** to stay in the air. Thrust, the force that moves a plane forward, is provided by a plane's engines.

The more thrust an engine provides, the faster the plane goes. This greater speed improves the lift on the aircraft. The faster the wings are moving through the air, the greater the difference in air pressure above and below them.

The four forces of flight

The arrows on this picture show the four forces of flight: lift, gravity, drag and thrust.

Lift

Drag

★

Thrust

Gravity

In level flight, lift is equal to the pull of gravity, and thrust is equal to drag if the speed is constant.

Drag, or **air resistance**, is another force acting on a plane. It is the force of friction* that occurs when something moves in air.

Drag increases as speed increases, so very fast aircraft are **streamlined** to reduce drag. A streamlined plane is designed so that air moves around it more smoothly.

Propellers provide thrust by pulling a plane through the air.

Jet engines provide thrust by pushing a plane through the air.

HOW PLANES ARE CONTROLLED

A plane needs to be able to move up and down, and to turn and bank (tip) to each side. To do this, the wings and tail are fitted with hinged flaps. These are known as **control surfaces**. They are made up of **ailerons** on the wings, and **elevators** and a **rudder** on the tail. By using a particular control surface, a pilot increases the drag on that part of the plane. This pushes it into a new position, as shown in the diagrams below.

How control surfaces work

— Aileron

Rudder

Elevator —

When turning, a plane also banks. This is called **rolling**. It is controlled by the ailerons on the wings.

Turning to the left or right is called **yawing**, and is controlled by the rudder on the tail fin.

Moving up and down is called **pitching**. Elevators on the tailplane control this.

This Airbus is just about to land. As the pilot controls the jet's descent, its ailerons, elevators and rudder are constantly twitching up and down or back and forth.

Big passenger jets have three or four engines.

The engine's thrust is reduced little by little so that the plane loses lift. Gradually, it comes down to the ground.

Big jets like this have their wheels, or undercarriage, tucked away during flights. This reduces the drag on the plane.

Aileron. The next time you fly, look for these moving on the backs of the wings.

See for yourself

You can create an airfoil wing with a strip of paper 6in x 2in and a pencil.

Fold the strip in half with the short edges together. Then move one edge back so that it is about ½in from the other edge and tape it down. This will make an airfoil. Slide it onto a pencil, as shown.

Put the edge that hangs over the pencil close to your lips. Blow steadily over the top of the fold. The difference in air flow above and below the wing makes it rise.

Blow here.

Wing rises.

Keep blowing over top of fold. —

Internet links

Go to **www.usborne-quicklinks.com** for links to the following Web sites:

Web site 1 Investigate flight at the Web site of the National Air and Space Museum.

Web site 2 Lots of information about flight, with links to other sites.

Web site 3 The principles of flight explained.

Web site 4 Find out about aerodynamics on this comprehensive and well-designed site.

Web site 5 An explanation of the forces that act on a paper plane.

AIRCRAFT DESIGN

The design of an aircraft depends on its function. Some planes need to be able to land on water, and some helicopters are used to lift huge weights. Here you can see some examples of different aircraft designs.

Tail fin

Tailplane

Rudder

Elevator

Body of plane, called **fuselage**

Seating for passengers

Passenger jet

This Boeing 747 is called a jumbo jet because of its size. It can carry up to 500 passengers.

Flight deck

Fuel tanks

Aileron

Radar equipment

Undercarriage (main landing gear)

Jet engines

Swing-wing plane

This Panavia Tornado is a swing-wing jet fighter. Its moveable wings can be straight (better for flying at slow speeds and landing) or swept-back (better for high-speed flying).

Wings sweep through this angle.

Sea plane

This Canadair CL-415 is a sea plane. It can take off and land on water. It floats because its body is shaped like a boat.

This plane also has wheels so it can move on land. Planes like this are called amphibians.

Supersonic passenger plane

Supersonic planes fly faster than the speed of sound. Concorde is the only supersonic passenger plane.

Concorde's delta-shaped wings (see page 145) help it to fly at speeds of up to 1,450mph.

"Invisible" plane

The Northrop B2 Stealth bomber's strange "flying wing" shape helps it to avoid radar detection. It has a wingspan of over 170ft.

The Stealth bomber is made of radar-absorbent materials.

Load-carrying helicopter

The Sikorsky Skycrane carries heavy loads to hard-to-reach places.

The Skycrane can carry the weight of over 150 people. Here, it is unloading a ready-made cabin to a building site.

FIRST FLIGHT

The first successful powered flight was made in 1903 by Flyer I. It was designed and built by the Wright brothers in the USA. The plane flew for about twelve seconds and lifted only a little way off the ground.

Cutaway showing wing structure

The Flyer I's wings were made of canvas stretched over a wooden frame.

HELICOPTERS

Helicopters can travel in any direction, or just hover in the air without moving. Their rotor blades are airfoils*, which provide lift as they spin around rapidly. To provide thrust*, the blades are tilted forward. They push the air behind them and this moves the helicopter forward.

This Robinson R22 has two main rotor blades. Some helicopters have three or four.

The tail blades keep the helicopter stable. Without them, it would spin around. The tail blades are also used for turning.

This helicopter does not have wheels, but rests on the ground on flat blades called **skids**.

JUMP JETS

The Harrier is a **Vertical Take Off and Landing** (VTOL) plane, or **jump jet**. It does not need a runway to take off.

A VTOL plane has thrusters which direct the power from its jet engines. In normal flight, the thrusters point to the back. This pushes the plane forward.

Thruster

This Harrier is taking off. Its thrusters point down at the ground, pushing the plane upward.

*Airfoil, Drag, Lift, Thrust, 44.

WING SHAPE

How fast a plane can go depends on the shape of its wings, as well as the size of its engines.

Straight wings give enough lift* for low-speed flying, with not much drag*.

Swept-back wings reduce drag at greater speeds, and are needed for larger-sized planes, such as passenger jets.

Delta-shaped wings enable an aircraft to fly at supersonic speeds. The fastest planes use this wing shape.

See for yourself

The wings on a model plane work in the same way as on a real plane.

You can make a paper plane of your own that can do turns and stunts. For a template, plus a step-by-step guide and flying tips, go to the Web site *www.usborne-quicklinks.com* and follow the instructions.

Internet links

Go to **www.usborne-quicklinks.com** for links to the following Web sites:

Web site 1 Find out more about the Wright brothers.

Web site 2 Discover how wind tunnels are used to design and test aircraft.

Web site 3 Read about how to make unusual flying objects.

Web site 4 The Web site of a plane manufacturer, with detailed descriptions and photos of its products.

Web site 5 Explore the Web site of another plane manufacturer.

ENGINES

Engines are machines that convert the energy stored in fuel into movement. They release the energy in fuel by **combustion**, that is, by burning it. This can take place outside the engine (**external combustion**) or inside the engine (**internal combustion**).

STEAM ENGINES

The first engines were **steam engines**. They were invented about 300 years ago, and used external combustion.

In a chamber outside the engine called the **furnace**, wood or coal was burned to boil water and produced steam. Because steam expands to take up to 2,000 times more space than water, it could be used to move a piston.

Piston

Cylinder

Early steam engine, built by Thomas Newcomen (1663-1729)

★

BETTER ENGINES

The earliest steam engines were not very reliable or efficient, but by the nineteenth century the technology had been improved and steam engines were being used to drive trains and power machinery in factories. James Watt (1736-1819) designed the widely-used steam engine shown here.

Pipe

James Watt's steam engine

Boiler

Belt

Cylinder (2)

Flywheel (5)

Furnace (1)

Condenser (3)

Sun-and-planet gear (4)

See for yourself

You can see the power of steam when a covered pan of water boils on a stove.

As the water boils, notice that the lid starts to bounce up and down. This is the expanding steam pushing against the lid.

Steam engines make use of this power to make things move.

1. To make this steam engine work, coal was burned in a furnace to heat water in the boiler.

2. A pipe carried steam from the boiler to the cylinder. The steam pushed a piston up inside the cylinder.

3. The condenser took used steam from the cylinder and the piston went down. The steam turned back into water.

4. A gear called a sun-and-planet gear converted the up-and-down movement of the piston into a rotating motion.

5. The flywheel rotated to power industrial machinery, to which it was connected by a belt.

TURBINES

Many modern power stations still use steam. Pressurized steam turns huge **turbines** – devices with rotating blades. This rotation generates electricity.

★ Electricity

Blades inside turbine are turned by force of steam.

Electricity is generated here.

Steam escapes here.

This is part of a huge steam turbine in a power station. The simplified diagram on the left shows how it works.

INTERNAL COMBUSTION

Internal combustion is more efficient than external combustion. **Internal combustion engines** burn a mixture of fuel and air inside the engine itself. This produces hot gases. These take up more space than the fuel and air they come from, and are used to create movement.

Modern cars have efficient internal combustion engines. In most cars, the engine drives the front wheels.

— Engine

EXHAUST FUMES

Some of the gases produced by combustion are poisonous. They leave the engine as **exhaust fumes**.

To reduce pollution, new car engines are fitted with **catalytic converters**. These contain **catalysts**, substances that can alter the speed of chemical reactions. The converter changes the poisonous exhaust fumes into less poisonous gases.

Cutaway view of metal catalyst

Harmful gases

★

Less harmful gases

In a catalytic converter, carbon monoxide is converted into carbon dioxide and water, and nitrogen oxide into nitrogen and oxygen.

Internet links

Go to **www.usborne-quicklinks.com** for links to the following Web sites:

Web site 1 Learn about some important steam engines, then play the steam engine games.

Web site 2 Information about famous steam pumping engines.

Web site 3 Find out how steam engines work.

Web site 4 Read about the history of steam engines, with pictures and animated diagrams.

Web site 5 See demonstrations of engines at work.

GAS ENGINES

Most car engines burn gasoline. **Gasoline engines** use internal combustion* to drive pistons up and down in hollow cylinders.

Each piston works in four stages called a **four-stroke combustion cycle**, as shown in the pictures on the right.

How a four-stroke engine works

Cylinder

Air and fuel

Piston

Spark plug

Fumes

1. Piston goes down, sucking a mixture of air and fuel into cylinder.

2. Piston goes up, compressing fuel and air mixture. This heats mixture.

3. Spark from spark plug ignites mixture. Gases expand and force piston down.

4. Piston rises again, pushing out remains of burned gases as exhaust fumes.

This is a four cylinder internal combustion car engine. It is built by Ford and called the Zetec.

Spark plug

A small spark is set off at this end of the plug.

DIESEL ENGINES

Diesel fuel is used mainly by larger vehicles and some trains. **Diesel engines** work in a similar way to gas engines, but at stroke one, only air is taken into the cylinder. This is compressed and heated to a very high temperature at stroke two. Diesel fuel is forced into the cylinder at stroke three, where it is so hot that the fuel burns without a spark.

This is the end of the crankshaft (see below).

One of the cylinders

One of the pistons

Transmission system of a rear-wheel drive car

(5)

Up-and-down movement of pistons (1) turns crankshaft (2).

Gears (3) connect crankshaft to drive shaft (4).

(4)

(3)

(1)

(2)

Drive shaft turns wheels through more gears, called the differential* (5).

TRANSMISSION

The four-stroke combustion cycle takes place in each of a car's cylinders. A series of shafts and gears, called the transmission, converts the up-and-down motion of the pistons into a rotating motion used to turn the wheels of the car. The system works in a similar way whether it drives the front or rear wheels of the car. (See also *Transmission* on page 53.)

* *Differential, 53; Internal combustion, 48.*

JET ENGINES

Jet engines are very powerful internal combustion engines* used by aircraft. The hot gases they produce are forced out of the back of the engine at high speeds. This pushes the plane through the air.

Jet engines are also known as **gas turbine engines** because the hot gases turn blades called turbines in the engine. The turbines suck air into the engine and compress it before it is mixed with fuel and burned.

TURBOJET ENGINES

The **turbojet engine** below is the simplest and fastest type of jet engine. It is noisy and less efficient with fuel than a turbofan engine (see right). Turbojet engines are only used for high-speed jet planes.

Cutaway of a turbojet engine

Air enters front of engine (1). Turbines in compression chamber (2) compress air. Compressed air is channelled into combustion chamber (3) and mixed with kerosene fuel. Mixture burns and produces hot, expanding gases.

(1)

(2)

(3)

(4)

Hot gases turn another turbine (4) as they pass through back of engine. This helps to drive compression turbines near front. Gases are forced out of exhaust tailpipe (5), pushing plane forward.

(5)

* Internal combustion engines, 49.

TURBOFAN ENGINES

Turbofan engines are not as fast as turbojets, but they are quieter and use less fuel. They are fitted to passenger jets.

Cutaway of a turbofan engine

Extra large fan at front (1) sucks in huge amounts of air. Some air goes through compression and combustion chambers (2), as in turbojet, producing hot expanding gases which are forced out of back (3).

(1)

(2)

(3)

(4)

Unlike turbojet, much of air goes around engine (4). It joins with gases at back, muffling noise and providing extra thrust.

There are two other kinds of gas turbine engine:

Turboprop

The power from the engine turns propellers that pull the plane through the air.

Turboshaft

Turboshaft engines are usually fitted to helicopters. The engine powers the main and tail rotor blades.

ROCKET ENGINES

Like jet engines, **rocket engines** produce hot gases which are forced out at great speeds. Instead of sucking in air for combustion, rocket engines carry liquid oxygen. This means that they can travel in space where there is no air.

Space rockets were developed from rocket missiles, such as this V-2 made in 1942.

Rocket fuel

Liquid oxygen tank

Rocket fuel and oxygen burn in the combustion chamber.

Hot gases shoot out of the exhaust.

See for yourself

Try this to give you an idea of how jet engines work. Thread some string through a straw and tie it tightly between two pieces of furniture. Blow up a balloon and hold the end so that it doesn't deflate. Ask a friend to tape the balloon to the straw.

Now let go of the balloon. The air rushes out and the balloon shoots forward.

Balloon

Straw

String

Internet links

Go to **www.usborne-quicklinks.com** for links to the following Web sites:

Web site 1 Learn about transmissions.

Web site 2 A links page, provided by NASA, to twelve sites connected with gas turbines.

Web site 3 Lots of information about jet engines.

Web site 4 An illustrated introduction to how gas turbines work.

CARS AND MOTORCYCLES

Cars, motorcycles and other road vehicles have transformed the way we live. They allow us to move from one place to another quickly and whenever we want to. But their popularity has led to problems of pollution and traffic jams. Car makers are constantly trying to develop cars that are less damaging to the environment.

This is one of the very first cars. It was built in Germany in 1885.

CAR TECHNOLOGY

The first cars were invented about 120 years ago. At first, they were slow, noisy, unreliable and dangerous. Since then, engineers and designers have refined all aspects of how cars work. These include making improvements to vital parts such as the engine, brakes, transmission and suspension. The vehicle below shows a good example of modern car design.

This cutaway car is a Ford Puma. It was first made in 1997 and has a top speed of around 125mph.

Laminated, shatterproof glass

Suspension

The hydraulic reservoir contains brake fluid.

Battery. This powers the electrical system.

Exhaust pipe under car takes fumes from engine.

Radiator fan. This keeps the engine cool.

Engine block

Disc brake

Drive shaft. This takes the power from the engine to the wheels.

ENGINE POWER

Internal combustion engines burn gasoline or diesel, creating gases that push pistons up and down in a cylinder. This motion creates the engine's power. The power is transferred from the engine to the drive shaft to the wheels, via the gear box, enabling the car to move. An engine's cylinders are measured in liters. A 1.4 liter car has cylinders that measure 1.4 liters in total.

Internal combustion engines, 49.

52

MOTORCYCLES

Motorcycles and cars share many features, although motorcycles don't need a differential (see below). Because they are relatively light, motorcycles can have engines as small as 50cm³ (50 cubic centimeters – half a liter). Bikes with very large engines are extremely powerful and can accelerate much faster than cars.

Rear indicator

Pillion seat

Low seat for low center of gravity*

Gas tank

Fairing (covering) reduces drag*.

Suspension

Exhaust

Disc brake

This Honda FireBlade has a 900cm³ engine.

Steel frame

TRANSMISSION

The **transmission** (see also page 50) is a system of **gears** that transmits an engine's power to the wheels. Gears are made of cogs (metal wheels with serrated edges called teeth). Engine power turns a rod called the input shaft, which is attached to one set of cogs. These turn another set of cogs which are attached to another rod – the output shaft. The output shaft turns drive shafts, which are attached to the wheels.

DIFFERENTIAL

The **differential** is a vital part of a car's transmission. It is a system of gears on the axles which allows the wheels to spin at different speeds. This is necessary for corners, when the outer wheels turn further and faster than the inner ones.

The inner wheel travels a shorter distance than the outer one. ★

SUSPENSION

Suspension is made up of two parts, a spring and a damper. The spring compresses and expands as the wheel goes over a bump. The damper delays the spring's action, so that the ride is not too bouncy.

The spring expands and contracts, moving a piston up and down a cylinder.

In the damper, oil is forced through valves, slowing down the piston. ★

BRAKES

Cars and motorcycles use **disc brakes**. When the brake pedal or lever is pressed, brake fluid is pushed down tubes, forcing brake pads to press against a disc in the wheel. The friction* causes the wheel to slow down.

Brake fluid is forced down pipes.

Fluid pushes brake pads against the disc.

Brake disc ★

See for yourself

To see how a differential works, use two pencils, two cotton reels, a strip of paper and some tape. Roll the paper around one pencil and secure it with tape. Slide it to the blunt end and insert the other pencil. Jam the sharp end of each pencil into a cotton reel. Paint a bright spot on each pencil.

As the "wheels" turn a corner, count how many times each pencil turns.

Internet links

Go to **www.usborne-quicklinks.com** for links to the following Web sites:

Web site 1 See detailed explanations and animations which show how the main parts of a car work.

Web site 2 Learn more about the history of cars, from their invention in the eighteenth century to the modern day.

Web sites 3–5 Three different sites that give up-to-the-minute news on the car industry.

Web site 6 An online magazine for classic cars and motorsport with lots of photos, news and special event features.

* Center of gravity, 33; Drag, 44; Friction, 26.

UNITS OF MEASUREMENT

Measuring things is one of the most important parts of science. There are two main measuring systems: **imperial** and **metric**. The imperial system is very old, dating from the twelfth century or earlier. The metric system was introduced in France in the 1790s. This is easier to use because it is based on the system of counting in tens – the decimal system.

IMPERIAL MEASUREMENTS

Length and distance

12 inches (")	= 1 foot (')
3 feet	= 1 yard (yd)
1,760 yards	= 1 mile
3 miles	= 1 league

Area

144 square inches	= 1 square foot
9 square feet	= 1 square yard
4,840 square yards	= 1 acre
640 acres	= 1 square mile

Mass

16 drams (dr)	= 1 ounce (oz)
16 ounces	= 1 pound (lb)
14 pounds	= 1 stone
160 stone	= 1 ton

Volume and capacity

1,728 cubic inches	= 1 cubic foot (ft³)
27 cubic feet	= 1 cubic yard (yd³)
5 fluid ounces (fl oz)	= 1 gill (gi)
20 fluid ounces* (USA: 16)	= 1 pint (pt)
2 pints	= 1 quart (qt)
4 quarts	= 1 gallon (gal)

* UK 1 fl oz = 0.0284 liters; USA 1 fl oz (liquid) = 0.0295 liters

METRIC MEASUREMENTS

Many metric measurements are spelled ending in "re" in British English and "er" in American English; for example, "metre" and "meter".

Length and distance

10 millimeters (mm)	= 1 centimeter (cm)
100 centimeters	= 1 meter (m)
1,000 meters	= 1 kilometer (km)

Area

100 square mm (mm²)	= 1 square cm (cm²)
10,000cm²	= 1 square m (m²)
10,000m²	= 1 hectare (ha)
100 hectares	= 1 square km (km²)

Mass

1,000 grams (g)	= 1 kilogram (kg)
1,000 kilograms	= 1 tonne (t)

Volume and capacity

1 cubic cm (cm³/cc)	= 1 milliliter (ml)
1,000 milliliters	= 1 litre (l)
1,000 liters	= 1 cubic meter (m³)

Scientists usually show numbers with up to four digits closed up, without commas, for example 9999. Numbers with more digits are shown with spaces to make them easier to read, for example 0.000 001. In non-technical writing, as in this book, numbers with over three digits are shown with commas.

CONVERSIONS

To convert between metric and imperial figures, use this table with a calculator.

To convert	into	multiply by
cm	inches	0.394
m	yards	1.094
km	miles	0.621
grams	ounces	0.035
kilograms	pounds	2.205
tonnes	tons	0.984
cm²	square inches	0.155
m²	square yards	1.196
km²	square miles	0.386
hectares	acres	2.471
liters	pints	1.76

To convert	into	multiply by
inches	cm	2.54
yards	m	0.914
miles	km	1.609
ounces	grams	28.35
pounds	kilograms	0.454
tons	tonnes	1.016
square inches	cm²	6.452
square yards	m²	0.836
square miles	km²	2.59
acres	hectares	0.405
pints	liters	0.5683

SI UNITS

SI units (short for the French *Système Internationale d'Unités*) are an internationally agreed system of units used for scientific purposes. The units have been defined very precisely in modern times. The meter, for example, is now defined as the distance light travels in a vacuum in $^1/_{299,792,458}$ of a second. Its measurement was originally based on a length of platinum alloy kept in Paris.

Quantity	SI unit
Length	meter (m)
Mass	kilogram (kg)
Time	second (s)
Temperature	kelvin (K)
Current	ampere (A)
Amount of a substance	mole (mol)
Light intensity	candela (cd)

DERIVED SI UNITS

These are derived from the units above using the equations shown.

Quantity	Derived SI unit	Equation
Area	square meter (m²)	Depends on shape
Volume	cubic meter (m³)	Depends on shape
Density	kilograms per cubic meter (kg/m³)	$\dfrac{\text{Mass (kg)}}{\text{Volume (m}^3)}$
Velocity	meters per second (m/s)	$\dfrac{\text{Distance moved (m)}}{\text{Time taken (s)}}$
Momentum	(kg m/s)	Mass (kg) x velocity (m/s)
Acceleration	meters per second per second (m/s²)	$\dfrac{\text{Change in velocity (m/s)}}{\text{Time taken for change (s)}}$
Power	watt (W)	$\dfrac{\text{Work done (J)}}{\text{Time (s)}}$
Force	newton (N)	Mass (kg) x acceleration (m/s²)
Energy/Work	joule (J)	Force (N) x distance moved in direction of force (m)
Pressure	pascal (Pa)	$\dfrac{\text{Force (N)}}{\text{Area (m}^2)}$
Frequency	hertz (Hz)	Number of cycles per second
Electric charge	coulomb (C)	Current (A) x time (s)
Voltage	volt (V)	$\dfrac{\text{Energy transferred (J)}}{\text{Charge (C)}}$
Resistance	ohm (Ω)	$\dfrac{\text{Voltage (V)}}{\text{Current (A)}}$

TEMPERATURE SCALES

There are three main scales for measuring temperature: the Fahrenheit scale (imperial), the Celsius scale (metric) and the absolute temperature scale (SI), which is measured in kelvins.

The absolute temperature scale is seen as the most scientific because 0 kelvin (-273°C) is **absolute zero**, the temperature at which no more heat can be extracted from an object. Scientific theory holds that this point of absolute cold would be impossible to reach in practice.

Celsius (°C)	Fahrenheit (°F)	Kelvin (K)
110	230	383
100	212	373
90	194	363
80	176	353
70	158	343
60	140	333
50	122	323
40	104	313
30	86	303
20	68	293
10	50	283
0	32	273
-10	14	263
-20	-4	253
-30	-22	243
-40	-40	233
-50	-58	223
-60	-76	213
-70	-94	203
-80	-112	193
-90	-130	183
-100	-148	173
-110	-166	163

CONVERSIONS

Convert	into	calculation
°C	°F	x9,÷5,+32
°C	K	+273
°F	°C	-32,x5,÷9
°F	K	-32,x5,÷9,+273
K	°C	-273
K	°F	-273,x9,÷5,+32

FACTS AND LISTS

PHYSICAL LAWS

Here is a summary of the key physical laws, for quick reference.

Newton's first law of motion (or principle of inertia) If an object is not being acted on by a force, it will either stay still or continue moving at a constant speed in a straight line.

Newton's second law of motion Any resultant force acting on an object will change its motion. How much the motion changes depends on the object's mass and the size of the resultant force.

Newton's third law of motion When an object A exerts a force on an object B, then B exerts an equal and opposite force on A.

Newton's law of universal gravitation There is a gravitational force of attraction between any two objects with mass, which depends on the masses of the objects and the distance between them.

Archimedes' principle The upthrust acting on an object is equal to the weight of the fluid that the object displaces.

Hooke's law The extension of a material is proportional to the force stretching it.

Law of conservation of energy Energy cannot be created or destroyed. It can only be changed into a different form.

Law of conservation of mass Matter cannot be created or destroyed in a chemical reaction.

Law of conservation of momentum After two objects collide, their total momentum remains the same (providing no other forces are acting on them).

HALF-LIVES

The half-life of a radioactive element is the amount of time taken on average for half the nuclei in a sample to decay. Each form of an element, called an isotope, has a different half-life. This can be millions of years or under a minute. Some examples are given below.

Name	Half-life
Uranium-238	4,500,000,000 years
Iodine-129	17,000,000 years
Thorium-230	80,000 years
Plutonium-239	24,000 years
Carbon-14	5,745 years
Strontium-90	29 years
Hydrogen-3	12.3 years
Cobalt-60	5.3 years
Sulfur-35	87.9 days
Phosphorus-32	14.3 days
Iodine-131	8 days
Radon-222	3.8 days
Lead-214	26.8 minutes
Thallium-210	1.32 minutes
Radium-221	30 seconds

WEB SITES

Go to **www.usborne-quicklinks** for links to the following Web sites:

General physics

Web site 1 A good source of information about many aspects of energy, forces and motion.

Web site 2 A useful study aid which covers the main areas of energy, forces and motion.

Web site 3 In-depth information about "The Physics of Matter, Energy, Motion and Forces", including magnetism, atoms, light, simple machines and more.

Web site 4 A Web site which explains physical laws and their applications.

Web site 5 Animated physics tutorials, with topics broken down into useful and logical lessons.

Web site 6 A selection of animated games and activities which demonstrate aspects of energy, forces and motion.

Web site 7 A Web site which answers the question "What is Physics?". It also provides a useful guide to what a physicist does, and how to become one.

Web site 8 A searchable database of questions which have been answered by a physicist. You can also submit your own physics question.

Scientists and discoveries

Web site 1 Lots of information about famous physicists and astronomers.

Web site 2 Meet the "Energy Heroes" – Thomas Edison, Allesandro Volta, Lewis Latimer and Nikola Tesla.

Web site 3 Visit this Web site for lots of facts about William Gilbert and his discovery that the Earth is magnetic.

Web site 4 A fascinating online Albert Einstein exhibit, covering his formative years as well as his major discoveries.

Web site 5 All about Robert Hooke, discoverer of the equation which defined elasticity.

Radiation

Web site 1 Visit this Web site to find out more about the modern uses of radioisotopes.

Web site 2 The American Institute of Physics Web site's excellent online exhibit about Marie Curie and the science of radioactivity.

Web site 3 Good information about carbon dating, the technique used to determine the age of ancient objects.

Web site 4 An introduction to nuclear science, including cosmic radiation.

SCIENTISTS AND DISCOVERIES

Ampère, André Marie (1775-1836) A French mathematician and physicist who did pioneering work on electricity and magnetism. The unit of electric current, the ampere, is named after him.

Aristotle (c.384-322BC) A Greek philosopher who made many contributions to physics, zoology and scientific theory.

Becquerel, Antoine (1852-1908) A French physicist who discovered radioactivity in 1896.

Brunel, Isambard Kingdom (1806-1859) This British engineer designed many great bridges and ocean-going steamships.

Celsius, Anders (1701-1744) This Swedish astronomer invented the first temperature scale to be divided into 100 degree units. It was named the Celsius scale.

Chadwick, James (1891-1974) An English physicist who worked on radioactivity and discovered the neutron.

Charles, Jacques (1746-1823) A French physicist who formulated Charles' law, which states the relationship between temperature and volume in gases.

Cugnot, Nicolas-Joseph (1725-1804) A French army engineer who in 1769 invented the steam tractor. This was the first vehicle to move on land by its own power.

Ford, Henry (1863-1947) An American automobile engineer who built the Ford Model T and pioneered mass-production techniques in industry.

Franklin, Benjamin (1706-1790) This American inventor and politician proved that lightning is a form of electricity.

Hooke, Robert (1635-1703) An English physicist and chemist who discovered the relationship between elasticity and force, as formulated by Hooke's law.

Joule, James (1818-1889) An English physicist who did important work on heat, and helped to establish the principle of the conservation of energy. The joule, a unit of measurement of work and energy, is named after him.

Meitner, Lise (1878-1968) This Austrian physicist explained nuclear fission for the first time in 1939. (See also *Hahn, Otto; Strassman, Fritz.*)

Newcomen, Thomas (1663-1729) An English inventor who built the first atmospheric steam engine.

Newton, Isaac (1642-1727) This English physicist and mathematician formulated fundamental laws of gravity and motion. He also discovered that light is made up of a spectrum of colors, and built the first reflecting telescope.

Pascal, Blaise (1623-1662) A French mathematician and physicist who made contributions to hydraulics and the study of atmospheric pressure. The SI unit of pressure, called the pascal, is named after him.

Röntgen, Wilhelm (1845-1923) This German physicist discovered X-rays in 1895.

Savery, Thomas (c.1650-1715) An English engineer who built the first steam engine.

Sikorsky, Igor (1889-1972) A Russian-born American aeronautical engineer who built the first successful helicopter in 1939.

Stephenson, George (1781-1848) An English inventor who invented the first successful steam locomotive in 1814 and, with his son Robert, built Stephenson's Rocket for the first passenger line in 1829.

Strassman, Fritz (1902-1980) A German chemist who, with Otto Hahn, discovered nuclear fission in 1938. (See also *Meitner, Lise.*)

Tesla, Nikola (1856-1943) A Croatian electrical engineer who invented the AC motor and high-voltage electrical generation.

Thomson, William (Lord Kelvin) (1824-1907) A British mathematician and physicist who did important work in thermodynamics, and established the absolute temperature scale.

Torricelli, Evangelista (1608-1647) An Italian physicist who devised the principle of the barometer in 1644.

Villard, Paul (1860-1934) This French physicist discovered gamma radiation in 1900.

Watt, James (1736-1819) A Scottish inventor who improved the steam engine and introduced the sun-and-planet gear. The watt, a unit of electrical power, is named after him.

Whittle, Frank (1907-1996) An English inventor who devised the jet engine in 1930.

Wright, Orville (1871-1948) and **Wilbur (1867-1912)** In 1903, these American brothers flew the first aircraft.

A-Z OF SCIENTIFIC TERMS

Absolute temperature scale The SI temperature scale, measured in kelvins (K), which are the size of degrees Celsius (°C). It places 100 kelvins between the ice point (273K) and the steam point (373K).

absolute zero The temperature at which no more heat can be removed from an object. Measured as 0K (-273°C).

acceleration A change in the velocity of an object, that is, in its speed or direction, or both per unit time.

acid rain Rain that has become more acidic after absorbing polluting gases such as sulfur dioxide and nitrogen dioxide.

aileron A control surface on a plane's wing used to direct turning and tipping (rolling).

airfoil The special wing shape, curved on top, flatter underneath, that creates lift.

air resistance See *drag*.

alpha particle A cluster of two protons and two neutrons emitted from the nuclei of the atoms of some radioactive substances.

alpha radiation A stream of alpha particles.

altitude Height above sea level.

atmosphere 1. The protective layer of air around the Earth that enables plants and animals to live. 2. The unit of atmospheric pressure at sea level.

atmospheric pressure The force of the air pressing down on a given area of the Earth's surface, divided by that area. At sea level, atmospheric pressure is one atmosphere (1 atm), also known as **standard pressure** and equivalent to 101,325 pascals.

atomic bomb A nuclear weapon that uses the power of nuclear fission.

atomic number The number of protons in the nucleus of an atom.

atoms The tiny particles from which elements are made. Each atom has a positively charged nucleus, consisting of protons and (except hydrogen) neutrons. This is usually balanced by enough orbiting negatively charged electrons to make the atom electrically neutral. See also *isotopes*.

Ball bearings Balls placed between two moving surfaces which reduce friction by reducing the amount of contact between the surfaces.

battery A store of chemical energy that can be converted to electrical energy.

beta particles High-energy electrons emitted when a neutron turns into a proton in the nucleus of a radioactive substance.

beta radiation A stream of beta particles.

bimetallic strip A strip made of different metals such as copper and iron fixed together, used in thermostats. When heated, the copper expands more than the iron, so the strip bends.

biogases Gases produced by rotting organic matter, used as fuel.

Calorie A unit of heat energy, equivalent to the amount of energy needed to raise the temperature of a gram of water by 1°C. It is equal to 4.2 joules. A kilocalorie, or Calorie (with a capital C), is 1,000 calories. Calories are often used instead of joules in calculations to do with energy release from food.

carbon An element found in all living things.

carbon dating A method of calculating the time that has passed since living matter died by measuring the level of radiation from carbon-14 present in the sample. See also *isotope; radioisotope.*

catalyst A substance that changes the rate of a chemical reaction but is itself left unchanged.

catalytic converter A device attached to cars which uses metal catalysts, for example platinum and rhodium, to remove toxic gases from the exhaust fumes.

Celsius scale A temperature scale which places 100 degrees Celsius (°C), between the ice point (at 0°C) and the steam point (at 100°C).

center of gravity The point at which the whole weight of an object seems to act.

centripetal force A force that keeps an object moving in a circle.

chemical energy Energy stored in a substance and released during a chemical reaction.

combustion The scientific term for all forms of burning. It releases heat and light energy.

conduction 1. The way heat energy is transferred in a solid by the vibration of the solid's heated particles. 2. The way an electric current is transferred in a substance by the movement of free electrons.

conductor A substance through which an electric current can flow, or heat can flow easily.

contact forces Forces that require two or more objects to be touching to take effect.

control surfaces Hinged flaps on a plane's wings and tail used to control the direction of its movement.

convection The main way heat energy is transferred in fluids (liquids and gases). The part of the fluid nearest the heat source expands, becomes less dense and rises, and the denser, cooler part sinks.

convection current A movement of a liquid or gas caused by convection.

Deceleration (or **negative acceleration**) A decrease in velocity in a given time divided by that time.

density The mass of a substance divided by its volume.

differential A part of a car's transmission which consists of gears on the axles which allow the wheels to go at different speeds.

drag (or **air resistance**) The force of friction that slows down objects moving in air.

dynamics The study of how forces affect movement.

dynamo See *generator.*

Effort The force needed to operate a machine.

elastic The term describing something that can be stretched out of shape or size by a force, but which returns to its original form when the force is removed (unless it exceeds its elastic limit). See also *plastic.*

elastic limit The point beyond which an elastic substance is altered, and weakened, permanently by stretching.

elastic potential energy (or **strain energy**) The potential energy an object has because it has been stretched or squashed.

electric charge A property of matter which causes electric forces between particles. Opposite charges attract, while like charges repel each other.

electric force The effect that electrically charged particles have on each other.

electromagnetic radiation (or **electromagnetic waves**) Energy waves made up of continually changing electric and magnetic fields, for example, light.

electron A negatively charged particle that moves around an atom's nucleus.

element A substance made up of atoms of the same type – all with the same atomic number. It cannot be broken down by a chemical reaction to form simpler substances. See also *isotopes.*

elevator A control surface on a plane's tail used to direct movement up and down (pitching).

energy chain A method, often pictorial, that shows how energy changes into different forms.

engine A machine which converts into movement the energy stored in fuel.

equilibrium The state of an object when the forces acting on it are balanced.

external combustion engine An engine which produces power from fuel burning outside its main body.

Fahrenheit scale A temperature scale which places 180 degrees Fahrenheit (°F), between the ice point (at 32°F) and the steam point (at 212°F).

field See *force field*.

fluid A liquid or gas.

force A push or pull on an object.

force field (or **field**) The area within which a force, such as a magnetic force, has an effect.

force magnifier A machine which overcomes a load greater than the effort it uses.

force ratio The load a machine needs to overcome divided by the effort.

fossil fuel A fuel such as coal, oil or natural gas, that is formed from the fossilized remains of plants or animals.

four-stroke combustion cycle The four-stage process by which the pistons in a vehicle's engine take in, compress, and ignite fuel, then release the exhaust.

frequency The number of waves passing a point in one second, measured in hertz (Hz).

friction The force that slows down moving objects that are touching.

fulcrum (or **pivot**) The fixed point around which something is turned.

fuselage The body of a plane.

Gamma radiation (**gamma rays**) Electromagnetic waves with the shortest wavelength and highest frequency. They are given off by radioactive substances.

gas turbine engine See *jet engine*.

gears A system of two or more cogs interlocking so that the motion of one controls the speed and turning effect of the other.

general theory of relativity A theory, developed by Albert Einstein, which related his special theory of relativity to gravity.

generator (or **dynamo**) A machine that converts kinetic energy into electricity.

geothermal energy Heat energy from underground rocks, used in some places to generate electricity. The rocks heat water underground, which is then pumped up and turned to steam which drives turbines.

global warming A rise in average temperatures around the world which scientists believe to be caused by the greenhouse effect.

gravitational field The area in which gravity has an effect.

gravity The pulling force that attracts objects to each other.

greenhouse effect The trapping of heat by carbon dioxide and other gases in the Earth's atmosphere.

gyroscope A wheel that spins very fast inside a freely moving frame, creating a centripetal force which enables it to tilt steeply without falling over.

Half-life The average time taken for half the radioactive atoms in a sample to decay.

hydraulic Powered by liquid pressure.

hydraulics The study of liquids in motion.

hydroelectric power Electricity generated by turbines driven by falling water.

hydrofoil A type of boat with stilts attached to underwater wings called **foils**. As it moves, the hull lifts out of the water, so water resistance is reduced.

hydrogen bomb A nuclear weapon that uses the power of nuclear fusion.

Ice point The temperature at which pure ice melts (273K; 0°C; 32°F).

inertia The tendency of objects to resist a change in their movement.

infrared radiation (**infrared rays**) Electromagnetic waves that are given out by anything hot.

instantaneous speed The speed of something at a given moment.

insulator A substance that cannot conduct electric current, or does not conduct heat well.

internal combustion engine An engine which produces power by burning fuel in an enclosed space inside.

internal energy The sum of the kinetic and potential energy of the particles in a substance.

isotopes Different forms of the same element. The atoms of each isotope have the same number of protons, but a different number of neutrons, in their nuclei. So isotopes of an element have the same atomic number, but different mass numbers. For example, carbon-12 has a mass number of 12 (and 6 neutrons in its nuclei), while carbon-14 has a mass number of 14 (and 8 neutrons).

Jet engine (or **gas turbine engine**) A powerful internal combustion engine used by aircraft. Air is sucked in through a fan, mixed with fuel and burned. The hot gas mixture turns turbine blades, and the gases are blasted out of the back of the engine at high speeds.

joule (J) The SI unit of energy and work.

Kelvin (**K**) The SI unit of temperature. See *absolute temperature scale*.

kilocalorie (or **Calorie**) See *calorie*.

kilojoule (**kJ**) 1,000 joules.

kinetic energy The energy an object has when it is in motion.

Lift The upward force of the air flowing under an airfoil shape such as that of an aircraft's wings.

load The force overcome by a machine.

lubricant A substance, such as oil, used to reduce friction.

Magnetism An invisible force that attracts certain metals, including iron.

mass The amount of matter contained in an object.

mass number The total number of protons and neutrons in the nucleus of an atom. The mass number of two atoms of the same element may be different, because they may be different isotopes.

millibar (**mb**) The unit of atmospheric pressure, equal to 100 pascals.

moment The turning effect of a force, measured in newton meters (Nm).

momentum A measure of an object's tendency to continue moving, equal to its mass multiplied by its velocity.

Negative acceleration See *deceleration*.

neutron A particle with no electric charge. Neutrons form part of the nuclei of every atom (except those of hydrogen).

newton (**N**) The SI unit of force.

newton meter (**Nm**) The unit of moment.

non-renewable fuels Fuels such as coal and oil, which can be used only once (see also *renewable fuels*).

nuclear energy The energy held in the nuclei of atoms.

nuclear fission A reaction in which an atom's nucleus is split open to form two or more new nuclei, releasing large amounts of energy.

nuclear fusion A reaction in which two small nuclei are joined to form a larger one, releasing large amounts of energy.

nuclear reactor The part of a nuclear power station, or nuclear-powered vessel, in which controlled nuclear fission reactions occur.

nuclear weapons Bombs that cause devastating explosions by releasing the energy of uncontrolled nuclear reactions.

nucleus The core section of an atom that contains protons and (except hydrogen) neutrons.

Pascal (**Pa**) The SI unit of pressure, equal to a force of one newton per square meter.

photon See *quantum theory*.

piston A cylindrical part that moves up and down inside a cylinder in an engine.

pitch Of a plane, to move up or down. Pitching is controlled by the elevators.

pivot See *fulcrum*.

plastic The term used to describe a substance which does not return to its original shape after stretching, but holds its new shape instead. See also *elastic*.

pneumatic Powered by the pressure of a gas, usually air.

potential difference (or **voltage**) The work needed to push a certain amount of electric charge between two points on a conducting pathway. It is measured in volts (V).

potential energy The energy an object has because of its position in a force field such as a gravitational field.

power The rate that work is done or energy is used, measured in watts (W).

pressure The force exerted over a given area by a solid, liquid or gas.

pressurized water reactor A nuclear reactor which uses the energy from nuclear fission reactions to boil water. This makes steam that drives turbines.

proton A positively charged particle in the nucleus of an atom. The number of protons determines the element.

pulley A machine that lifts heavy loads with a system of ropes passing around grooved wheels.

Quantum theory The idea that energy comes in tiny "packets", called **quanta**, which helps to explain the properties of electrons and the relationship of energy to matter. Quanta of electromagnetic radiation, such as light, are called **photons**.

quarks Particles which are believed to make up protons and neutrons.

Radiation Energy that travels in the form of electromagnetic waves, or as high-energy particles (as emitted by radioactive substances).

radioactive decay The process by which an unstable nucleus emits radiation, becoming the nucleus of a series of different elements, until stability is reached.

radioactive tracing A medical technique used to follow a substance through a patient's body by adding radioactive elements to it.

radioactivity The release of radiation from the nuclei of unstable atoms.

radioisotope A radioactive isotope.

radiotherapy A medical technique which uses controlled doses of radiation to kill cancer cells.

relative density The density of a substance in relation to the density of water.

relative velocity The velocity a moving object appears to have when viewed from another moving object.

relativity See *general theory of relativity* and *special theory of relativity*.

renewable energy resources Sources of energy such as the Sun, wind or water, that can be used to generate power without themselves being used up (see also *non-renewable fuels*).

resultant force The total effect of all the forces acting on an object.

rocket engine An engine similar to a jet engine, but rockets carry liquid oxygen for combustion, so they can travel in space where there is no air.

rudder A control surface at the rear of ships and planes which directs turning to the left and right (yawing).

Scalar quantity A quantity that has magnitude but no direction.

SI units An internationally agreed system of standard units used for scientific measurement.

solar cell A device that converts the Sun's energy into electricity.

solar collector An array of black panels which absorbs the Sun's heat and uses it to warm water in a central heating system.

solar energy The Sun's heat and light energy.

special theory of relativity A theory, developed by Albert Einstein, which deals with the relationship of the speed of light to the measurement of time and space, and the relationship of matter to energy.

specific heat capacity The amount of heat needed to raise the temperature of 1kg of a substance by 1K.

speed The measure of how fast an object is moving, calculated as the distance it travels in a certain amount of time.

speed of light The speed at which light travels in a vacuum – about 300,000 kilometers per second.

speed of sound The speed at which sound travels – measured in dry air at 0°C as 331 meters per second.

spring balance A device which uses a spring to measure a force (in newtons).

standard pressure See *atmospheric pressure*.

steam engine The earliest kind of engine, based on external combustion, which boils water, producing steam that drives pistons.

steam point The temperature of steam above water boiling at atmospheric pressure (373K; 100°C; 212°F).

strain energy See *elastic potential energy*.

streamlining A way of designing vehicles so that air flows over them in smooth lines, reducing drag.

supersonic speed Any speed greater than the speed of sound.

suspension A system of springs in a vehicle that absorbs the effects of an uneven road surface.

Terminal velocity The maximum velocity reached by a falling object, at which point acceleration ceases, and velocity is constant.

thermal capacity The amount of heat needed to raise the temperature of an object by one kelvin.

thermodynamics The study of energy changes involving heat.

thermostat A device that switches an electric circuit on and off in response to a change in temperature. See also *bimetallic strip*.

thrust The force that moves a plane or rocket forwards.

transmission A system of gears that transmits the engine's power to the wheels of a vehicle.

turbine A machine with a shaft and blades, which are turned, for example, by the force of wind or steam. The movement (kinetic) energy is converted to electricity.

turbofan engine A type of jet engine with an extra-large fan. They are slower than turbojets, but quieter and more efficient.

turbojet engine The fastest type of jet engine, used in high-speed jet planes.

turboprop engine A jet engine that drives propellers to power an aircraft.

turboshaft engine A jet engine that powers the rotor blades in a helicopter.

Upthrust The force of a fluid pushing up on an object inside it.

Vacuum An empty space where there are no particles of air or other matter.

vector quantity A quantity that has magnitude and direction.

velocity The speed an object travels in a particular direction.

voltage See *potential difference*.

volume The amount of space an object occupies.

VTOL Of a plane, Vertical Take Off and Landing. Such planes take off directly upwards and so do not need runways.

Watt (W) The SI unit of power.

weight A measure of the strength of the pull of gravity on an object.

work Work is done when a force moves an object. It involves a transfer of energy and is measured in joules. One joule equals the work done when a force of one newton moves an object one meter.

Yawing Of a plane or ship, turning to the left or right. It is controlled by the rudder.

TEST YOURSELF

1. Energy is measured in units called:
A. watts
B. joules
C. kilograms *(Page 12)*

2. The boiling point of water is:
A. 32°F
B. 100°C
C. 212°C *(Page 13)*

3. Which statement is true?
A. convection never occurs in solids
B. convection only occurs in liquids
C. conduction never occurs in solids *(Pages 14-15)*

4. An alpha particle is made up of:
A. two protons and two neutrons
B. two protons
C. a high-speed electron *(Page 16)*

5. Radioactive carbon-14 is written as: $^{14}_{6}C$. This form of carbon has
A. six protons and six neutrons
B. six protons and eight neutrons
C. fourteen protons *(Page 17)*

6. A force's strength is measured in:
A. kilograms
B. meters
C. newtons *(Page 21)*

7. A force is:
A. a vector quantity
B. a scalar quantity
C. neither a vector nor a scalar quantity *(Page 21)*

This digram shows the forces acting on a wheelbarrow.

Which arrow represents

8. the force of the ground on the wheelbarrow? *(Page 23)*

9. the force of the man on the wheelbarrow? *(Page 23)*

10. the weight of the wheelbarrow? *(Page 23)*

11. It is easier to turn something around a fulcrum if the force is applied:
A. a long distance from the fulcrum
B. very close to the fulcrum
C. at the fulcrum *(Page 23)*

12. If no forces are acting on a moving object, the object will:
A. slow down and stop
B. continue moving at the same speed in a straight line
C. change direction *(Page 24)*

13. Whenever you push an object you will always feel:
A. a push in the opposite direction
B. a push in the same direction
C. no push at all *(Page 24)*

14. When a book slides across a table, the force that slows it down is called:
A. lubrication
B. drag
C. friction *(Page 26)*

15. Average speed is equal to:
A. distance multiplied by time
B. time divided by distance
C. distance divided by time *(Page 28)*

16. The difference between speed and velocity is that:
A. speed is a scalar quantity whereas velocity is a vector quantity
B. speed is a vector quantity whereas velocity is a scalar quantity
C. they have different units *(Page 29)*

17. If an object accelerates, then its:
A. speed and direction must change
B. speed or direction must change
C. speed must increase *(Page 29)*

18. An apple falling from a tree is: pulled downward because of
A. the pull of gravity on the apple
B. the apple's low center of gravity
C. the smooth skin of the apple, which reduces friction *(Page 32)*

19. Which statement is true?
A. the mass of an object depends on the pull of gravity on that object
B. mass is measured in newtons
C. the weight of an object is due to the pull of gravity of the Earth on that object *(Pages 32-33)*

20. Which statement is true?
A. a force acting over an area exerts pressure
B. the pressure of a needle is small due to the small area of the point
C. hydraulic machines are driven by gas pressure *(Pages 34-35)*

21. Atmospheric pressure:
A. is at its lowest near to the ground
B. increases with height above ground
C. is due to the weight of air pressing down *(Page 34)*

22. When using a lever:
A. the point about which the lever turns is called the fulcrum
B. the force you apply is the load
C. the force you need to overcome is called the effort *(Page 36)*

23. Which statement is correct?
A. a man doing work gains energy
B. work is only done when a force makes an object move
C. work and power are both measured in watts *(Page 39)*

24. Ships made of steel float because:
A. steel is less dense than water
B. the hollow space inside the ship makes it less dense than water
C. the upthrust of the water on the ship is less than the weight of the ship *(Page 41)*

This diagram shows three of the four forces acting on an airplane.

Which arrow represents

25. the lift? *(Page 44)*

26. the airplane's weight? *(Page 44)*

27. the drag? *(Page 44)*

28. In the diagram above, the missing force is the:
A. pull of the Earth's gravity
B. thrust provided by the engines
C. centripetal force *(Page 44)*

29. In level flight, lift is equal to the
A. speed of the airplane
B. pull of gravity
C. air resistance *(Page 44)*

30. Wings that are curved on top and flatter underneath are called:
A. hydrofoils
B. airfoils
C. ailerons *(Page 44)*

Answers
1.B 2.B 3.A 4.A 5.B 6.C 7.A 8.A 9.C 10.B 11.A 12.B 13.A 14.C 15.C 16.A 17.B 18.A 19.C 20.A 21.C 22.A 23.B 24.B 25.B 26.A 27.C 28.B 29.B 30.B

61

INDEX

You will find the main explanations of terms in the index on the pages shown in bold type. It may be useful to look at the other pages for further information.

ACKNOWLEDGEMENTS

PHOTO CREDITS
(t = top, m = middle, b = bottom, l = left, r = right)

Corbis: **2-3** Richard T. Nowitz; **6-7** Joseph Sohm, ChromoSohm, Inc; **10-11** Sean Aidan, Eye Ubiquitous; **14-15** (main) Gary Braasch; **17** (b) Owen Franken; **18-19** (main) Bettmann; **21** (main) Robert Landau; **49** (main) Richard Hamilton Smith.
© **Digital Vision**: **1**; **4-5**; **8** (t), (b); **9** (bl); **12** (l); **14** (l), (bm); **15** (tr); **19** (ml); **20** (tr); **22**; **25** (tm), (tr); **26**; **28** (t), (br); **30** (t), (b); **34** (tr), (bl); **40-41** (t); **42-43**; **44-45**.
NASA: **27** (l)
Science Photo Library: **32** (b) Science Photo Library;
35 (tr) Will & Deni McIntyre; **37** (main) Jeremy Walker.
Ford Motor Co Ltd 27 (tr); **36** (r); **49** (ml); **50** (m); **52-53**;
Goodyear GB Ltd 26 (l); **Honda UK 53** (tr); **Northern Lites 34** (m);
Porsche Cars Great Britain 29 (bm); **Snow and Rock 26** (br).
Tony Stone: **cover** Robin Smith

ILLUSTRATORS
Simone Abel, Sophie Allington, Rex Archer, Paul Bambrick, Jeremy Banks, John Barker, Andrew Beckett, Joyce Bee, Stephen Bennett, Mark Bergin, Roland Berry, Gary Bines, Isabel Bowring, Trevor Boyer, John Brettoner, Peter Bull, Hilary Burn, Andy Burton, Terry Callcut, Kuo Kang Chen, Stephen Conlin, Sydney Cornfield, Dan Courtney, Steve Cross, Gordon Davies, Peter Dennis, Richard Draper, Brin Edwards, Wayne Ford, John Francis, Mark Franklin, Nigel Frey, Stephen Gardener, Peter Geissler, Nick Gibbard, William Giles, David Goldston, Peter Goodwin, Jeremy Gower, Teri Gower, Terry Hadler, Alan Harris, Nick Hawken, Nicholas Hewetson, Christine Howes, John Hutchinson, Ian Jackson, Hans Jessen, Karen Johnson, Richard Johnson, Elaine Keenan, Frank Kennard, Aziz Khan, Stephen Kirk, Richard Lewington, Brian Lewis, Jason Lewis, Steve Lings, Rachel Lockwood, Kevin Lyles, Chris Lyon, Kevin Maddison, Janos Marffy, Andy Martin, Josephine Martin, Rob McCaig, Joseph McEwan, David McGrail, Malcolm McGregor, Dee McLean, David Mead, Annabel Milne, Robert Morton, Louise Nevet, Martin Newton, Louise Nixon, Steve Page, Justine Peek, Maurice Pledger, Mick Posen, Russell Punter, David Quinn, Barry Raynor, Mark Roberts, Michael Roffe, Michelle Ross, John Russell, Michael Saunders, John Scorey, John Shackell, Chris Shields, David Slinn, Guy Smith, Peter Stebbing, Stuart Trotter, Robert Walster, Craig Warwick, Ross Watton, Phil Weare, Hans Wiborg-Jenssen, Sean Wilkinson, Ann Winterbottom, Gerald Wood, David Wright, Steve Wright.

American editor: Carrie A. Seay